DATE DUE

CHANGING EAST-WEST RELATIONS AND THE UNITY OF THE WEST

Changing
East-West Relations
and the Unity of the West

Papers presented to the European-American Colloquium, May 1 and 2, 1964, at the Washington
Center of Foreign Policy Research, School of Advanced International Studies, The Johns Hopkins
University

Edited by
ARNOLD WOLFERS

THE JOHNS HOPKINS PRESS, BALTIMORE

Acknowledgments

The Center acknowledges with special gratitude the generous support from The New World Foundation and The Ford Foundation that made possible the Colloquium and this publication.

Preface

As part of the celebrations with which the School of Advanced International Studies of The Johns Hopkins University dedicated its new building on Massachusetts Avenue, The Washington Center of Foreign Policy Research, an affiliate of the School, convoked a European-American Colloquium on "Changing East-West Relations and the Unity of the West." Forty specialists in the field of international relations, almost half of them from Europe, were invited to meet in Washington on May 1 and 2, 1964, to discuss the papers now published as essays in this volume. The publication was decided upon because the analyses by the authors, very enlightening to the conferees, should prove of equally intense interest to a wider public.

It stands to reason that any marked change in the relationship between the Western nations and the Soviet Union, their most powerful adversary, would be a matter of greatest concern to the peoples on both sides of the Atlantic, whether because of the promise it might offer for more peaceful conditions in the world or because of the dangers it might create to vital Western interests. But has such a change occurred? There seems to be agreement among the authors that some change is taking place and that it is pointing toward a relaxation of tension which the French, with convenient brevity, call a détente. As they probe into the chief aspects of such a détente, the essays reveal how controversial the subject is, even among specialists, and not solely between Americans and Europeans. There is conflict of views on the very existence and nature of an easing of tension and differences of opinion are hardly less marked when it comes to deciding what the motivations are that lie behind what at the time of writing and with serious qualifications can pass as a Soviet détente policy. And what will relaxed tensions of some duration do to the strength and unity of the West and what consequences should the Atlantic nations draw in order to be ready to cope with the changing environment? More of a consensus could have been expected if it were merely a matter of agreeing on the existence of facts, though some of them are hard enough to get at when it comes to penetrating the veil of Communist secrecy and the screen of Communist deception. But what is at stake here is the formulation of plausible hypotheses on the relationship between the future course of Soviet foreign policy and such diverse and controversial factors as the psychology of Soviet leaders, the economic conditions prevailing in the Soviet Union, or the balance of world forces.

This collection of essays deals consecutively, and in logical sequence I believe, first with the existence and nature of the détente, then with at least one of the possible causes for a change in Soviet attitude and behavior, then with the impact of reduced tension on Central Europe—focal area of the East-West confrontation—and, finally, with the consequences for future Western behavior.

The first two essays deal with what at the very least is a lull in the acute struggle between East and West that characterized the periods of the Berlin and Cuban crises. The emphasis is on the real or alleged *rapprochement* between the United States and the Soviet Union that is throwing its shadow over the entire area of the Cold War, if only because of the hopes and fears it generates. The reader who places the first two essays side by side may be struck by the apparent effect that differences in philosophy, temperament, and personal experience have on the interpretations and prognostications of two men—one British, the other American—who are both exceptionally knowledgeable on international relations. While the first essay stresses the promising elements of change which, however slim at this time, may be harbingers of greater change in the future, the second focuses on the persistent features in the adversary relationship with the Soviet Union which, even in the face of alterations in mood, require unerring persistence in the policy of strength and firmness that has served the West so well in the face of an exacting struggle with a powerful and expansionist foe.

If there was nothing more substantial to go on than hunches about the inner workings of Mr. Khrushchev's mind, there would be little point to inquiring what the chances are that a Soviet policy of relaxation constitutes more than a passing atmospheric change or a temporary shift in methods of policy of the kind that have occurred more than once before. But, may not more tangible and objective factors have come into play which, by exerting pressure, are forcing the Soviet leaders to mend their fences in the West? The authors of essays three and four, specialists on Soviet and Red Chinese affairs, respectively, were asked to concentrate on one such factor, the Sino-Soviet rift, a new and spectacular factor that marks the failure of Soviet leadership to hold the supposedly monolithic Communist world together. However, the two essays show that the rift is far more the effect than the cause of Soviet détente efforts in the West. The Chinese launched their ideological attack against Khrushchev out of fear, shared by more than a few Europeans, that the two superpowers, in order to ban the danger of a nuclear confrontation between each other, were preparing to enter into agreements, if not at the expense, then at least without the foreknowledge of their allies. Yet, whatever the origins of the rift, it cannot fail to strengthen Khrushchev's interest in a détente if, as several of the authors stress, Soviet policy is guided by estimates of the world balance of forces. The emergence of a hostile power in the place formerly occupied by Soviet Russia's major ally in the East has shifted the balance against the Soviet Union.

Several of the authors argue that the Cuban missile crisis marked the beginning of the current Soviet détente strategy because it upset Khrushchev's estimate of the balance of world forces. They see the Soviet leaders awakening in the days of Cuba to the inadequacy of Soviet military might for any direct confrontation with the United States. If they are right and if cold calculations of power supply the key to the present Soviet interest in a relaxation of tension, an important conclusion can be drawn at least for the way the West should *not* respond to the Soviets, assuming it desires continued relaxation: it would be pursuing incompatible policies if it downgraded and weakened its armaments and alliances and thereby gave Khrushchev reason to revise his estimate of the world balance once again and this time in the opposite direction; it would be pulling the rug from under his strategy of détente.

Before moving on to the last three essays, it is worth adding that the third essay, which deals with Soviet affairs, discusses another objective factor that might in time lead to change, if not in Soviet purposes, then at least in the priorities attached to them. This factor is internal to the Soviet Union and consists of changes occurring within Soviet society. If these changes should be turning the minds of the new economic and administrative elites and of the people at large away from ideology and toward material tasks, the zeal of the Soviet party hierarchy to revolutionize the world in the name of communism might, as the Chinese leaders suspect, not survive for long.

With the discussion shifting from the causes to the effects on Western unity of a relaxation of East-West tensions, it makes sense to concentrate on Central Europe, the area most sensitive to even the faintest signs of a possible Soviet-American *rapprochement*. Germans, particularly, may well conclude that the best, if not the only, chance of agreement between two relatively equal adversaries like the two superpowers lies in their common acceptance of the status quo which, in the case of Germany, means acceptance of her partition. The authors of essays five and six, one German, the other American, are wide apart in their views on what the Western nations, including Germany, should do in the face of the problem thus posed. The chief reason for their disagreement—and for that of many others inside and outside of Germany who think as they do—arises from a divergent evaluation of two evils. Those who regard the status quo as intolerable prefer to see continue the state of high tension which, after all, has not proved disastrous, to stabilizing and legitimizing a hateful and unjust order; but those who consider the hazards of grave tension unbearable because of the risk of mutual nuclear destruction urge Germany to consent to the concessions that may have to be made if there is to be agreement with the Soviets. The latter tend to overlook that this option, if interpreted as a sign of weakness or if fatal to the solidarity of the Western alliance, may destroy the détente rather than to advance the cause of a more stable peace.

The last three essays may seem to deviate from the main topic, but that is not the case. Assuming a situation of changing East-West relations, these authors are asking what the United States and its friends in Europe, neutral as well as allied, can and should do to be prepared for the challenges of a changing environment. All three have some criticism to offer concerning the way the United States has led the Alliance in its confrontation with the Soviet Union, saying, for instance, that American policy has paid too little heed to the European clamor for emancipation from U.S. tutelage—for which Charles de Gaulle is only the most potent spokesman—or that it failed to unite the Western coalition behind a common strategy and common purposes, or that the U.S. has insisted too rigidly on the neat pattern of a grand design and on hastily erected structures. However, none of the three authors, it should be noted, reproaches the United States either for an excessive zeal to maintain military strength or for an excessive fervor in the pursuit of a policy of détente. One may conclude from this that neither the Frenchman nor the neutral Swiss nor the American—whom de Gaulle would label an Anglo-Saxon—despair of pursuing simultaneously two objectives which in pure logic look incompatible but which imaginative statesmanship should be able to harmonize: convincing the Germans that nothing precious to them will be sacrificed for the sake of diminishing the anxieties of their allies and demonstrating beyond the doubt of even the most anxious that no opportunity will be missed for seeking fair and practical settlements with the Soviet Union.

These essays may not show the way of accomplishing what looks like squaring the circle, but they will have served a useful purpose if they alert the reader to the difficulties and complexities of the task ahead and thereby help restrain inclinations toward complacency or wishful thinking.

Washington, D. C.   ARNOLD WOLFERS
July, 1964

Contents

Relaxation of East-West Tension and Its Effect Upon the West

by
Kenneth Younger*

I

International tension is bad. This must be the position from which discussion starts, and the onus of proof must lie on those who seek to water down or contravert this bald statement. Tension results from the clash of interest between states, from fear and suspicion, from high levels of armaments, and from all the various conditions which combine to cause international conflict and war. In so far as relaxation of tension is the opposite of this, it is a natural objective of rational statesmanship, especially in the age of nuclear weapons.

Some qualifications immediately spring to mind. Relaxation of tension may be based on deception and may amount to no more than a stratagem whereby a victim's

---

* *Kenneth Younger:* Labor Member of Parliament from 1945 to 1959 and Parliamentary Secretary to the Home Office and Minister of State for Foreign Affairs in Clement Attlee's government from 1947 to 1951. Since 1959 he has been Director of the Royal Institute of International Affairs, London.

suspicions are allayed so as to make him an easier prey. Or again, the relaxation, though genuine, may be purchased at too high a price, leading to the sacrifice of just causes or legitimate interests. In any dispute, therefore, it is necessary to form a judgment about the adversary's basic intentions, to decide whether there is irreconcilable hostility or merely a passing clash of interests, and whether the adversary's attitude can best be altered by courting his good will through compromise or by seeking to weaken him till he gives way.

Generalizations of this kind help to define the issue, but they cannot provide any easy rule of thumb for statesmen. There is no substitute for the exercise of intelligence and judgment in each particular case. Two features of the current tension between East and West, which at present means primarily between the United States and the Soviet Union, distinguish it from the general run of conflicts between great powers. Firstly the ideological element is greater than it has been at any time since the wars of religion; and secondly, the stakes are higher, on account of nuclear weapons, than they have been in any previous period of history. Both of these have a bearing upon the problem of the relaxation of tension, but the latter is the more significant and will be considered first.

Ever since the Franco-Prussian War of 1870 inaugurated the era of wars between industrial states, the stakes have been rapidly rising and with them the deterrent effect of the threat of war. The change introduced by nuclear weapons in this respect has added a new dimension to strategic thinking, to the point where the existing nuclear powers are already agreed that nuclear war cannot be the instrument of any rational policy. Though Chinese utterances have indicated a bolder attitude toward the risks which may be taken in the nuclear age, there is no reason to suppose that, by the time that China is herself a nuclear power, she will in the last resort be any more willing than

the United States and the Soviet Union to embark upon a
nuclear war in order to obtain her political ends.

It may therefore be claimed that the great powers already recognize a mutual interest in keeping the tension
between them below the point at which it involves serious
risk of nuclear war. Differences of opinion as to where
this point is gives rise to the practice of brinkmanship,
the application of which has already alarmed the world
on more than one occasion. But however near the brink
statesmen may think fit to go, it seems improbable that
they will ever voluntarily cross it as a matter of deliberate policy. Though this proposition does not exclude the
possibility of mistake, it is, if true, something new in history.

The limited restraint upon international tension, imposed by the danger of nuclear war, has not yet shown any
sign of contributing to the settlement of the numerous disputes which are, cumulatively, the main reason why
tension exists between East and West. On the contrary,
it is arguable that some of the more acute situations, such
as Berlin, Cuba, or Quemoy and Matsu might, in pre-
nuclear times, have been resolved one way or another by
some combination of force and diplomacy, whereas today
they linger on in frozen immobility because, now that the
ultimate sanction of military force is ruled out by the
nuclear stalemate, the traditional incentive to compromise
is also absent. Accordingly, the tension due to the various
specific disputes is stubbornly maintained by both sides
at what one might call subnuclear level, while, simultaneously, laborious efforts are made to keep the tension
from increasing to the point where thoughts might begin
to turn to the threat to use nuclear weapons. Berlin pro-
vides, perhaps, the best instance of tension which has been
both long sustained and also, since 1949, carefully kept
from reaching crisis pitch.

The long-drawn-out conversations conducted after 1961

between Mr. Rusk and Mr. Gromyko were the diplomatic product of this situation. Every aspect of the Cold War was, one is told, surveyed. At various times fear was voiced in the West that such talks could end only in some form of appeasement or, if they failed, in even higher tension. In fact they appear to have produced no significant change in the positions of either power on any of the subjects which were in dispute between them. To that extent, they were a failure. Yet they were also accompanied by a certain over-all relaxation of East-West tension and may have contributed to it. Rightly or wrongly they gave the impression that they represented the first recognition by both sides that contact must be maintained on all subjects, however immediately unpromising, so that sudden and dangerous surprises might be avoided.

But despite the talks dangerous surprise followed in the shape of the Cuban crisis of 1962. This was just the sort of occurrence which had always been feared by those who think the relaxation of East-West tension dangerous. There is no need, for the purposes of the present discussion, to analyze the motives which led to the Cuban affair or to allot blame. It is enough to recall that the general trend of Soviet policy, including presumably what was said in the private Rusk-Gromyko talks, had seemed to be moving away from provocative or dangerous initiatives. This was no doubt one reason why the United States' intelligence authorities were not at first inclined to credit reports which were reaching them about the installation of Soviet missile bases in Cuba. The Cuban crisis showed that it is perfectly possible for a policy of relaxation of tension to be pursued at one level, while all the time a highly dangerous policy is being pursued at another. In this instance the risk taken was of a kind which immediately aroused the fear of nuclear war.

It is, of course, uncertain how near the world really came to nuclear war on this occasion. As the event proved, it was always open to the Soviet government, having taken the risk, to make sure of avoiding war by withdrawal, and Mr. Khrushchev may well have decided from the outset that this was what he would do if necessary. Nevertheless, the Cuban experience was bound to create doubts in the minds of Western leaders about the value of a so-called relaxation of tension which amounts only to a manner-of-speaking and is not based on any significant concessions on matters in dispute.

Despite the force of this reasoning, it is possible to argue that the sequel to Cuba points in a rather different direction. When the immediate crisis was past, it was widely feared that tension would rise dangerously high and that, in particular, it might be transferred to Berlin, where local conditions might have seemed more favorable to the Soviet Union than they were in Cuba.

Instead, the opposite happened. It soon became clear that the Soviet government was concerned to take advantage of the escape route which President Kennedy's controlled firmness had left open for her. Tension was allowed to fall. In due course East-West conversations were renewed and produced their first achievement, the nuclear test-ban treaty.

Disappointing as this treaty was, in the sense that it did not fulfill the hope that it would pave the way for a system of mutual arms inspection, it was the first formal expression of a common interest between the United States and the Soviet Union in the control of nuclear weapons. Though it cannot yet be asserted that this is being reflected in progress in the disarmament negotiations at Geneva, there is some evidence that the need to avoid provocation of the other side (another way of describing a relaxation of tension) may be beginning to be more widely accepted by the leading powers in the framing of their own defense policies. The correct lesson to be learned from the Cuban crisis may therefore be not that the relax-

ation of tension proved to be a dangerous fraud, but rather
that it taught the nuclear powers that the policy of limiting tension must now be applied to particular disputes as
well as to the problems of the military balance, if the risk
of war is to be avoided.

Despite the growing feeling that East-West relations
may be about to improve, there are numerous disputes
around the world which show no sign of moving toward
solution. Vietnam, Cuba, Cyprus, and many other areas
see the United States and Soviet Union heavily involved
on opposite sides in situations which seem likely to get
worse before they are better. Current Soviet attitudes to
the new West German government also seem designed to
renew tension over the German problem—though not,
significantly, over Berlin, where the risks may well be
judged too great.

Many of these situations are not strictly of Soviet making, but are examples of the Soviet Union's ability to take
advantage of the instability which is inseparable from the
search for a new equilibrium after the liquidation of the
European empires. It is normal that the United States
and the Soviet Union should find themselves on opposite
sides in nearly all these matters, primarily because of the
Soviet Union's ideological commitment to steer every
revolutionary situation toward a Communist solution. This
commitment is likely to be maintained for a considerable
time, partly because it offers the Soviet Union an obvious
method of extending her influence in the world as against
the non-Communist powers, and partly because any repudiation of her revolutionary mission would play into the
hands of her Communist rival, China.

There is therefore little reason to expect an early relaxation of the tensions arising from this kind of cause. Mr.
Khrushchev and other Soviet spokesmen have virtually
said this on the many occasions when they have insisted
that there can be no let-up in the ideological conflict and

have expressly reasserted their right and duty to give
their fullest support to just wars of liberation. The concept of "relaxation of tension," as understood in Moscow,
is thus a somewhat limited one. From the Soviet point of
view the current U.S. attitude to the possible growth of
communism in the Americas must seem to imply an
equally rigid ideological position.

II

In so far as there is still a division of opinion in the West
about the way to handle this situation, it boils down increasingly to a question of timing. There is no longer
significant support either for the early Dulles aim of roll-
ing back the Communist tide from Communist countries,
with the bomb in one hand and the Bible in the other, or
for the overoptimistic belief that Communist powers are
little more than liberal agrarian reformers who are going
through a difficult phase in their development. Both these
extremes are now out.

All sensible men now accept that Soviet society is changing rapidly and that this is beginning to have international
consequences, which are accentuated by the rift with
China. But they also see that the only important change
in Soviet policy which has so far actually occurred is the
repudiation of nuclear war as an instrument of policy.
All Soviet objectives remain as they were and seem likely,
for the reasons already given, to be maintained in the
foreseeable future. The question for the West is therefore
to judge at what speed and on what issues Soviet policy
is evolving toward a genuine toleration of non-Communist systems and an acceptance of something less than
complete victory as its eventual aim in the ideological
struggle. At some point it may be possible for the West
to encourage and speed up this evolution by moving some
distance toward Soviet points of view.

As already stated, it is in the field of nuclear armaments that Soviet acceptance of something less than complete victory is already evident. It is therefore in arms
control and disarmament that active negotiation seems
most likely to meet with some response and to lead to a
genuine lowering of tension. This proposition clearly does
not imply that unilateral concessions are to be expected
from either side, but simply that the cautious and continuing pursuit of what is now recognized as a common
interest has a good chance of resulting in some limitation
of the arms race and some avoidance of risks, even if, for
a time, disarmament itself eludes the negotiators.

On other issues it is harder to identify points on which
genuine compromises are now possible. Berlin seems the
least likely of all the major disputes to yield to this treatment. But in some areas, such as Southeast Asia, where
the local desire for a position of nonalignment is strong,
there may be a hope of pacification by the acceptance of
some form of neutralism. Western policy has already
been forced to accept this for Laos and Cambodia and
may yet, for want of any attainable alternative, have to
contemplate it for Vietnam and, eventually, for the whole
area, including Malaysia and Indonesia. Here the weight
of early Western mistakes lies heavily upon Western
policy-makers. Looking far ahead, the chances of achieving stability in this area on the basis of United States'
support for wholehearted hostility to China seem very
poor indeed. Just as an early French compromise with
Ho-Chi-Minh after 1945 might by now have produced a
"Tito-ist" Vietnam, with which the West could live in
peace, so today relaxation of tension, even at some immediate cost, may prove to be the West's least risky
option.

In the whole area from India to Japan, one of the main
obstacles to constructive diplomacy has been, and still is,
the emotional commitment of the United States to a

Chinese policy which isolates her from her major allies. This reflection raises at once the question of the correct attitude to be adopted in the West to the normalization of relations with Communist countries. On this there has always been some difference of emphasis among the Western allies, and in some cases sharp disagreement. In the extreme cases of China and more recently of Cuba, United States policies have seemed to aim at achieving a position as close as possible to a state of war, but without the essential element of military operations. "No diplomatic recognition, no trade and virtually no unofficial contacts" has been the formula for relations between these countries and the United States, whose allies have been pushed as far in the same direction as American pressure can push them. In another area, the German Federal Republic has, for more readily intelligible reasons, insisted on a rather similar attitude toward East Germany, and this special case has colored her attitude to the rest of Eastern Europe.

With other Communist countries, including the Soviet Union, a much more normal relationship has been generally accepted among the Western allies, and serious disputes have been, on the whole, limited to questions of East-West trade, the embargo on strategic goods, and the granting of credits. It cannot be denied that the differences of opinion on these questions have been partly due to commercial considerations. Countries like Britain, whose foreign trade forms a high proportion of her total economic activity, are more reluctant to restrict trade with the Communist bloc on political grounds than the United States, whose commercial stake is relatively insignificant. But in addition to this there has been, during much of the postwar period, an underlying conflict between two views about the evolution of the Communist threat.

According to one view, more strongly held in the immediate postwar decade than today, Communist regimes should be weakened in every possible way. Not only should military supplies be withheld from them—a proposition on which there is little or no dispute—but everything possible should be done to hold back their economic development, thus making it hard for them to allocate adequate resources to armaments. This view in turn depends upon the belief, for which all too much support can be found in Soviet speeches, that the world consists of two "camps" whose conflict is inevitable, so that anything which is good for one must automatically be bad for the other.

The natural deduction from this view is that high tension between East and West is useful, since the object is to overstrain the adversary until his hostile effort begins to flag. It is a weakness of this policy that the means, short of war, for weakening an area which covers half the world are so limited as to seem almost negligible as an instrument of victory. Its more likely effect is to encourage the construction of a war economy within the Communist area and to reduce the interest, already unhealthily small, which Communist countries feel in maintaining a measure of commercial interdependence with the rest of the world. This result can seem good only to those who have already given up hope of any eventual accommodation with an undefeated Communist bloc.

The other view is that, over the long haul, improved living standards and a more relaxed way of life in Communist countries will be advantageous to the non-Communist world as well. This view can be made to seem naive when it is taken to imply that increased wealth more or less automatically blunts the aggressiveness of a society or nation. No such generalization is tenable. In particular the last hundred years of Japanese and German history could be more easily quoted as proof of the contrary proposition.

Nevertheless, the argument has some special attraction in the context of East-West rivalry today. For the Soviet Union is not simply an old-style expansionist power seeking either the direct domination of larger territories, like a medieval monarch, or new markets and raw materials, like a nineteenth-century imperialist. As already stated, Soviet objectives have a higher ideological content than this and depend, at least partly, on the belief both that communism is historically destined to become a world-wide system and that capitalist powers are bound to seek its overthrow by all available means.

Already this century-old formula corresponds too little to the observable state of the world to command the unquestioning belief it once did. Easier living in Communist countries, coupled with a normalization of their relations with the rest of the world, seem to provide the best hope of gradually reducing further the sharpness of East-West antagonisms. This, rather than an eventual defeat of communism through its collapse in countries where it is established, is surely the object to be sought, and the method of seeking it must include a cautious but sincere pursuit of relaxation of tension between the blocs.

III

One way to test the soundness of this thesis is to consider what alternative courses are in fact open to the West, in a situation where "the other side" is showing a willingness to encourage a lower state of tension and a desire to avoid the risk of major war, but not, as yet, to pay any substantial price for this in terms of concessions over particular disputes.

What has been argued so far has been that the West has little choice but to respond in kind and has in fact an interest in doing so. That is to say the West should be ready to talk to the East on all issues, but without any intention of surrendering vital positions; that the search for common ground over disarmament and arms control should continue unceasingly; and that increased commercial and cultural contacts, and all other aids to the normalization of relations with Communist states, should be promoted.

It has not been claimed that these policies are likely to lead to quick settlements, but rather that they will have a tendency, over a long period, to encourage the sort of political and social evolution within the Communist bloc which would make eventual agreement possible to contemplate, and that they will diminish the risk of some sudden catastrophe owing to misunderstanding by one side of the other's motives. This last point is, perhaps, the only one which is already valid in relation to China as well as to the Soviet Union. China does not yet seem to be prepared for the kind of contacts and discussions with the West that are already an accepted part of Soviet policy; but at least it is better policy for the West to maximize contact with China, for instance through common membership of international organizations, than deliberately to foster conditions which can only produce mutual ignorance and perhaps unnecessary misunderstandings.

One alternative policy for the West would be to refuse discussions with the East on the ground that no progress toward agreement is possible—in other words, to glare silently at the other side across an Iron Curtain or a Berlin Wall. It is hard to see what constructive merits can be claimed for such an attitude. If, as is often argued, a policy of détente produces few results, this alternative, surely, is calculated to produce none at all. It is also calculated to reduce to a minimum the already inadequate sources of information on which the West has to assess the realities of Soviet policy.

Another alternative might be to maintain constant pressure upon the other side, by means which are not easily defined but may be presumed to include hostile propaganda and possibly subversion. It is particularly in relation to the German problem that this course is sometimes recommended by limited sections of German opinion. That Germans should unremittingly seek for ways of obtaining from the Soviet Union the reunification of their country and a solution for Berlin is very natural and is accepted by all their allies. But to imagine that a hardening of the East-West barrier or the maintenance of East-West tension can contribute toward these aims is to ignore the most elementary implications of the nuclear age. For it has never been conceivable, at least since the launching of the first Sputnik, that the reunification of Germany could be extracted from a weak but irreconcilably hostile Soviet Union. The only context in which legitimate German aspirations have any hope of realization is one in which détente between East and West in Central Europe has reached a point where the maintenance of the present unnatural division no longer seems to the Soviet and other Eastern governments to be essential to their security.

The policy of those German circles who argue against détente virtually excludes the possibility of such a favorable conjunction ever being reached. It also overlooks the common interest, which Germany shares with all her other allies, in insuring that tensions are kept below the level that would bring increased risk of nuclear war. There is nothing more irritating, or more potentially dangerous, than the impression which these German circles contrive to give that Germany would wish the United States to take greater risks in her nuclear diplomacy than she herself is willing to contemplate. Nothing could be further from the truth, and no country would stand to lose more by any such switch of American policy than Germany.

What is no doubt true is that Germans have a special interest in avoiding any risk that the status quo in Germany might become formally sanctified as the result of a bargaining process carried on primarily between Washington and Moscow. If East-West détente were to mean a détente to be enjoyed by others at the price of legitimate German interests, which her allies have for many years professed to have adopted as their own, then there would be a genuine German grievance. But there is not a shred of evidence, after several years of experience with the so-called policy of détente, that United States or Western policy has included any tendency of this kind. So far from this being the case, the policy of movement to which Dr. Erhard and Dr. Schroeder subscribe, along with other Western leaders, seems to be the only one which can prevent the status quo in Europe from becoming effectively frozen, and it therefore keeps alive the hope that East-West relations in Central Europe will one day evolve to the point where the German problem, at present manifestly insoluble, may find an acceptable outcome.

IV

One of the anxieties expressed both in the United States and, less often, in Europe, is that a policy of détente may impair the unity of the Western Alliance. It is no doubt true that if an alliance is formed, as NATO was, to meet an external threat, any slackening of the threat is liable to relax correspondingly the bonds which hold the allies together. But it is wrong to describe this as the consequence of a policy of détente.

If the various governments which are joined in an alliance become less fearful than they were of the danger that brought them together, the sense of détente will be there and cannot be removed by any artificial attempt, either to pretend that it is not, or to insist on the rigid maintenance of alliance policies, which were appropriate only when the

fear was greater. In so far as there is evidence of disunity
within the Western Alliance at the present time, it is due
partly to the fact that the fear of massive Soviet aggression in Europe has decreased and partly to doubt about
the protection afforded by the Alliance, now that the
United States has become for the first time vulnerable to
nuclear attack. It has little or nothing to do with such
efforts as have been made in recent years to reduce tension between East and West by a process of continuous
negotiation. Indeed, in present circumstances any suggestion that negotiation should be avoided in order to maintain allied unity, would certainly disrupt Western unity by
making people feel that the Alliance was being made an
end in itself instead of a means for dealing with a genuine
threat.

The same argument applies to the question, which every
government faces, of persuading the public to accept the
cost and the other sacrifices involved in the maintenance
of adequate defense. It is often said that the vagaries of
public opinion in the democracies put them at a serious
disadvantage, and that talk of détente is liable for that
reason to lead to a premature slackening of the Western
defense effort. Recent history offers little support for
these apprehensions. There has in fact been no failure of
public will in defense in any of the major Western countries where very great defense burdens have been accepted
by national parliaments. What has sometimes failed is leadership, and any weaknesses which exist in NATO at the
present time are due to this. Where a clear lead is given
and the need for any particular level of defense is com-
petently and honestly explained, the public response is
usually adequate; but any suspicion that the international
dangers were being deliberately exaggerated in order to
secure increased defense appropriations would be as coun-
terproductive with public and parliamentary opinion as in
the field of allied unity. As Mr. Roswell Gilpatric has re-

cently written,[1] the United States cannot afford deliberately to avoid seeking the reduction of tensions in order to keep the public alert to dangers, any more than it can afford to ignore dangers where they exist, in order to build support for a policy of peaceful accommodation. Other allied countries are in precisely the same situation.

The only sane attitude for democratic governments to adopt is to make the best judgment they can about the real dangers and then to ask their people to support whatever measures are appropriate to that judgment. One of the great contributions that President Kennedy made to the conduct of foreign policy was the impression he gave of basing his decisions upon the most objective assessment of information which he could obtain and of presenting this clearly to the public. In this he moved away from government by myth and by hunch and toward a more rational diplomacy backed by a public whose common sense he was prepared to trust. This is the example which should be followed.

The difference between those who resist the idea of détente between East and West and those who are prepared to work toward it lies less in their estimate of the enemy than in their faith in their own moral fiber and that of their allies. A sound policy leaves no room for the artificial maintenance of tensions for fear that one's own will power may prove unequal to the temptations of relaxation. If a great country or a great alliance allows its confidence in its people and its forms of government to sink to this level, it is likely to lose the ideological battle in any event.

[1] *Foreign Affairs,* April, 1964.

Détente:
Effects on the Alliance

by

*Charles Burton Marshall**

The Line of Argument

My view, though that of an American centering on
United States policy, is not to be taken as *the* American
view. Quite the contrary, I have grave doubts concerning some of the modes of thought and action in vogue with
my own government. Of more than one vaunted achievement I may say, quoting Edmund Burke, "I have no man's
proxy. I speak only for myself, when I disclaim, as I do
with all possible earnestness, all communion with the ac-
tors in that triumph, or with the admirers of it." [1]

The topic concerns détente. A synonym is relaxation of
tensions. The expressions, applied to international affairs,
convey a cumulative process abating confrontation and
contest, making intractable issues tractable by lowering
their gravity, and finally rechanneling the flow of events

---

* *Charles Burton Marshall:* Formerly consultant, Committee on
Foreign Affairs, United States House of Representatives; member of
Policy Planning Staff, Department of State; and Political Advisor to
the Prime Minister of Pakistan. Author of *Limits of Foreign Policy.*
[1] Edmund Burke, *Reflections on the Revolution in France* (London:
Oxford University Press, 1951), pp. 92–93.

from distrust to confidence and from confliction to compatibility.

Détente is neutral as an abstraction. The process is subject to being judged good or bad only by taking account of issues in contention. Tensions are merely symptoms of opposed purposes. To appraise tension between or among diverse entities, one should have to know what they are respectively trying to do. Accommodation is inseparable from the question of what is to be accommodated.

Here specifically the scope concerns relations with the Soviet Union. Essentially the focus is on conditions of peace with respect to Europe. The topic is inseparable from a set of specific undertakings regarding Europe, pre-eminently the North Atlantic Alliance. The subject inherently involves interactions between the quest of détente and the Alliance. That thought sets the focus and content of this essay.

My main points are these:

The hopes raised during World War II and its immediate sequel for a reliable world order resting on a scheme for collective security premised on continuity of the prevailing coalition and objectified in the Charter of the United Nations foundered on an array of divisive issues of dominion pre-eminently involving the disposition of Germany.

The North Atlantic Treaty, growing out of frustration of that hope, substituted regional defense for universal collective security.

Though not free of problems and issues in this respect, it has worked as a framework for the military security of the area, developing in response to unfolding demands of the situation. A highly significant event in this course has been the inclusion of the German Federal Republic in the scheme of military—and, as a corollary, political—collaboration.

Beyond the defensive purpose, the Alliance was intended to create conditions to render the adversary amenable to an acceptable settlement in Europe. In this respect, the undertaking of the Alliance implicitly represented, at least in the American view, not abandonment but deferment of hope for world concord as a basis for peace. The Alliance was, and remains, ambiguous regarding modes and conditions for such a settlement.

The urge for détente, reflecting lingering fascination with that hope, accentuates relevant ambiguities in the Alliance. The crux of the problem of settlement remains the disposition of Germany.

The effect is disintegrative. The danger is that of impairing the Alliance, even dismantling it, by premature and ill-considered gestures toward détente. The outcome is all too likely to be loss of the Alliance without gain of a settlement.

For those interested in pursuing the questions, the arguments are elaborated in four sections focusing in order on the following themes:

Interplay between the immediate aim of regional security and ultimate hopes for accommodation with the adversary in the origin of the alliance.

The alliance's course with respect to regional security.

The lingering problem of accommodation with the adversary.

The prospects and the price of accommodation.

*Interplay between the Immediate Aim of Regional
Security and Ultimate Hopes for Accommodation with
the Adversary in the Origin of the Alliance*

To begin the account, it is fitting to call to mind assumptions dominant in policy preceding formation of the North Atlantic Alliance. Policy was premised on an expectation of continuity, as a basis for an enduring peace, of the coalition prevailing in the war. This expectation was epitomized in the United Nations. Issues regarding conditions of peace over the globe would be handled by a Security Council inclusive of the principal elements of the victorious combination—namely, the United States, the Soviet Union, the United Kingdom, France, and China—as permanent participants. In essence the scheme involved applying on a world scale an analogue to the historic Concert of Europe, with great powers joining hands to guide lesser ones, to restrain irresponsibles, and to tranquilize the Balkans wherever located. Resolving and acting in unison, the permanent members would presumably dispose power enough to pacify the world, but under the organization's rules this power was to be checked and mitigated by a requirement of concurrence by two of a quota of six other and lesser governments taking turns as members.

It was a collective security system of sorts—with central direction, calculable resources, and a presumed capacity to make joint plans for meeting contingencies—a collective security arrangement with teeth, in a phrase of art. Like the Concert of Europe, the scheme depended on a huge prerequisite—that of unanimity among its major elements, and in particular between the pre-eminent two, in this case the United States and the Soviet Union.

Hope, however, had apparent grounds even beyond that optimism perennially disposed to discern a dawn of universal reason. In confrontation with common foes, the major elements had had experience in disposing political, military, and economic power to agreed ends. Repeatedly agreement between the United States and the Soviet Union had proved determinative, and the others had been impelled to go along. Problems of handling erstwhile enemies would provide an irreducible necessity of continued collaboration. The agony of war, moreover, was believed to have been enough to drive the world sane. Ideologies were supposed to have burned out under the searing effect of battle. Concurrence in seeing the ultimate folly of risking another such holocaust would provide a solvent for animosities and impel the leading members to work together as allies.

With no longer a common foe to confront in battle, the assumed unity proved to be a fragile reality. At once cracks began to show in the foundation. Relations with ex-enemy countries, notably Germany, gave rise to divisive issues rather than unifying interests. Improvisation has saved the organization, but the original design for the Security Council has not been fulfilled in practice.

Following disappointment in this venture to organize peace globally, the United States' policy has had to adapt to a view of possibilities more finite than the dream of a universal solution. It has done so without retreating to a simple and circumscribed view of responsibility like the one reinvoked in the sequel to World War I. The venture has involved reconciliation to a role as a leading protagonist in a deep and persistent contest and the putting aside of a traditional inhibition about alliances—a part of the national psyche reaching back to a time when Americans, as yet colonial subjects of the Crown, were anxious both to enjoy protection afforded by British power and to avoid embroilment in the mother country's quarrels and rivalries.

Among terms associated with international affairs, *alliance* is a good way from being the most precise. In eighteenth-century usage the term broadly denoted an arrangement for mutual benefit and limited participation among states.[2] Later usage narrowed its meaning to a contract between or among governments more or less explicitly obliging at least one of them to use military force beyond its own domain, under certain defined contingencies which indicate the purpose and scope of the obligation, against an adversary or adversaries, whether or not specified, external to the undertaking. One might appropriately apply the term in this sense to the organized unity among permanent members of the Security Council predicated in the Charter as the foundation for universal collective security. An alliance thus conceived as a central frame of collaboration in ministering a world assumed to be basically harmonious well suits an old American dream. Combinations against adversaries in a tense and contentious world are a quite different matter. Alliance in this version is alliance undiluted, alliance in the balance-of-power motif, alliance charged with the perplexities warned against in Washington's and Jefferson's famous admonitions to America.

At the inception of the subject alliance, most of the countries concerned across the Atlantic were only beginning to rally from the depletions of war and the indignities of occupation. Their public life had suffered impairment. Their economies still faltered. Their military establishments were in bad order or, in some cases, even virtually nonexistent.

A formidable Soviet military presence, which held mastery over Eastern Europe and pushed well into Central Europe, pressed heavily upon them. The Communist attachment of Czechoslovakia by coup stood fresh in their minds as an example of what they might expect in event of having to face Soviet power alone. The Berlin blockade demonstrated the intransigence of Soviet designs. The

[2] Felix Gilbert, *To the Farewell Address* (Princeton: Princeton University Press, 1961), pp. 44–45.

internal programs of indigenous Communist parties indicated the extent of adversary intentions.

With U.S. assistance, these countries were just under way in a combined effort of economic rehabilitation. The corollary of a common effort in military security followed as logically as the idea of a fence goes along with the idea of a cornfield. A purely European combination—exemplified in the Brussels Pact of 1948 among the United Kingdom, France, Belgium, the Netherlands, and Luxembourg —simply did not add up to enough to do the job, for it only combined factors of weakness. An arrangement of mutual defense—one spanning the Atlantic and embracing initially the United States, Canada, Iceland, the United Kingdom, Norway, Denmark, Belgium, the Netherlands, Luxembourg, France, Italy, and Portugal—followed in natural course.

The fundamental character of the shift from striving to organize peace on a basis of world concord to trying to realize and to protect it by regional combinations was obscured, however, in the United States government's appreciation and interpretation of its own actions.

True enough, the scheme in the Charter had not panned out—the circumstance accounting for the new undertakings. "Whenever a powerful minority repudiates the basic principles and uses the procedures to accomplish directly contrary purposes or to frustrate the organization, then obviously it will not work as intended," Secretary of State Dean Acheson explained in the hearings on the North Atlantic Treaty. This, however, was no reproach to the concept—a sound fraternity with, alas, some bad brothers in it. The Secretary's rationalization dealt with the United Nations as a mechanism rather than a society. The machine was ideal, irreproachable. The whole fault was in wayward hands put to the wheel.[3] The dream was valid in every respect save relation to reality.

To explain regional defense as an auxiliary to rather than a substitute for universal collective security, much was made of Article 51 of the Charter itself as a provision countenancing regional defensive pacts and of parallels of language concerning goals contained in the respective basic documents. These links to the Charter were cited in answer to a Senator who sought rebuttal of charges "that this is a military alliance" and assurance against any similarity to "balances of power and things like that in the old world . . . commonly denominated military alliances." [4]

The United States' representative to the United Nations, Warren R. Austin, labored the denial with considerable explicitness:

> I have been asked whether the North Atlantic Treaty is not the resumption of the practice of setting up a power equilibrium. . . . My answer is "No."
>
> The ancient theory of balance of power lost its potential utility through the voluntary association of states, on the basis of sovereign equality and universality. The old veteran, balance of power, was given a blue discharge when the United Nations was formed. The undertakings of the peoples of the United Nations to combine their efforts through the international organization to maintain international peace and security, and to that end, to take effective collective measures, introduced formally the element of preponderance of power for peace. And out went old man balance of power.[5]

---

[3] *North Atlantic Treaty: Hearings before the Committee on Foreign Relations, United States Senate, Eighty-first Congress, First Session* (Washington: Government Printing Office, 1949), p. 7.

[4] *Ibid.*, p. 14.

[5] *Ibid.*, p. 97.

Reaffirming a view that "Military alliances are not in the tradition of the United States," the Secretary of Defense, Louis Johnson, described the North Atlantic undertaking as "not a foreign military alliance in the customary sense." This denial, representing an attempt by officials to assure themselves as well as the public against the fearsome idea of acting in a mode from the bad old world instead of the good new one, was a recurring theme in the exposition. The olden and alien alliances, as to which the new project was presented in favorable contrast, were not specified or analyzed. The substance of the distinction was left unclear.

All split hairs notwithstanding, the North Atlantic Treaty was, and remains, a design for maintaining security by working on and combining factors of armed power within an exclusory scope. In Secretary Johnson's own words:

> From the military viewpoint, the basic objectives of the collective defense system are to deter war and to attain maximum military effectiveness in war, if war cannot be prevented. The North Atlantic Treaty will form a basis for improving United States security by improving the military potential of all the member nations. This potential will be improved in terms of collective action as well as individual armed strength.[6]

An obligation to respond in event of attack on any party in its homeland or in insular positions in the North Atlantic was made pervasive and explicit upon each member. Each was left free to determine its own response. The principle of collaboration in strategic preplanning was avowed and institutionalized, however, among members not equal in potential—some contributing significant positions rather than appreciable manpower or other deployable military resources. The strategic anchor was the United States' monopoly of nuclear weapons, then deliver-

---

[6] *Ibid.*, p. 146.

able solely by bombers. Of a relatively rudimentary type, these weapons were numerous enough for inflicting huge damage, though not enough for annihilating enemy establishment in event of general war. The cover afforded by their capacity for retaliation was extended to the selected parts of Europe as well as North America. This capability was to be supplemented by conventional forces generated mainly in Europe, with some American subvention, to provide a respectable impediment to attack from the East. Operational facility was to be enhanced by drawing the participant lands together into one area for planning, maneuver, and operations.

The European participants were thus to be restored in confidence by being assimilated into a strategic, going concern—by knowledge of having now, westward across the Atlantic, a reserve area of great potential—while the United States in turn added great depth to its territorial defenses. The aim was redress with respect to capabilities for bringing force to bear and the reassuring and intimidatory effects of these capabilities on friends and adversaries. Even a Humpty Dumpty might find it difficult to make words reflect a significant differentiation between this focus and the balance-of-power concept.

Besides revealing an inhibition about departing from tradition, the asserted distinctions between the new undertakings and old-time alliances, examined in context, reflect a purpose to disavow belligerent intentions and to stress peaceable aims. The Alliance was originated to support peace in a minimal sense—meaning absence of destructive use of force—and to save participating governments from the baleful necessity of having to choose between submission and hostilities. Beyond that aim, the Alliance was conceived also as a step toward peace in its broader sense of a reliable legitimate order—meaning a disposition of authority and jurisdiction enjoying general acknowledgment of its rightfulness and enabling all affected by it to feel confident of its unchallenged continuation into a long calculable future.

The Alliance was to do its work in this last respect by laying a basis for bringing the adversary to an accommodating disposition in a prolonged process of conversion. Confronted by situations of strength, in the prevailing phrase of art, Communist power would presumably be rendered amenable eventually to settled arrangements compatible with outside interests—that is to say, the United States' and her allies'. The Communist side was to be persuaded by irreducible realities to see matters in perspectives which had been hopefully attributed to the Soviet regime in the engrossing design for an enduring peace developed in World War II and embodied in the Charter. Thus the Alliance would fulfill its purpose by remedying the conditions giving rise to it. By frustrating the adversary, it would transform him. These goals inherently involve a question of how—by whom and in accord with what criteria—to decide when they have been reached.

As part of the supreme law of the land in the United States the Alliance was given place along with a quite distinguishable scheme for establishing security on a chimerical basis of a global concert of power. Rapport and collaboration between the great powers of the Atlantic area, especially the United States and the Soviet Union, were conditions necessary to realization of the global concert. The absence of these conditions was what necessitated the regional Alliance. The obligations entailed by the latter undertaking, however, were made absolute only for a term of twenty years—this in deference to the United States' preference as distinguished from the European allies' wish for a fifty-year period[7]—so that any member may leave on a year's notice from 1969 on. In contrast, the Charter has no terminal date. The solid, measurable

---

[7] *Ibid.*, p. 87.

reality was thus made contingent, whereas the dream was made enduring.

The Alliance's Course with Respect to Regional Security

Three states of mind, broadly speaking, are relevant in measuring the avail of the Alliance as a military undertaking for preserving peace in its minimal sense—the putative opponents', our allies', and then our own. Confidence on our side is a function of doubt on the Communist side, where, obversely, the estimate of opportunity varies in proportion to disbelief among the allies in the efficacy of the Alliance. All parties concerned must go through a sort of continuous notional warfare involving calculation of interrelationships among these states of mind. The United States' primary concern necessarily focuses on adversary estimates, because basically the other side holds the franchise on the question of success or failure of the deterrent design. Yet this adversary's estimate is inseparable from calculation of will within and among Alliance members. This brings us to the relationship between the concept of deterrence and strategy—two aspects of the same matter. The deterrent design is to render unlikely the occasion for having to put the military strategy to a test. Deterrence can work only on a basis of high estimate of the effectiveness of the strategy in event of a failure of its primary aim of deterrence. Thus, one is not excused from burdens of military analysis by hope of never having to test relevant capabilities against adversary forces.

In the instance of the Atlantic Alliance, these rudimentary considerations are complicated by certain characteristics of contemporary weaponry, which does not quite match anything in other and more familiar lines of experience. Analogies recurringly drawn between the deterrent-strategic link and poker, football, or the operations of fire departments, and so on, never quite fit. Even the now familiar metaphor about deadly scorpions co-existing in a bottle is inadequate. The problems must be understood in their own terms. The novel problems in calculation revolve around the prodigious destructive capabilities of contemporary weapons of top-level potential, their instant readiness, and great radius of feasible delivery. Effects and countereffects cannot be tested in experience. There is no really adequate way of running maneuvers with them. So men are left to compute and to theorize about them.

Computation and theorizing, moreover, must struggle with problems arising from an enormous and continuous multiplication of offensive power—that is, of prodigious capabilities in contemporary specialized weapons for destruction in carrying on attack as distinguished from suitability for interdicting attack. The advantage of the offensive over the defensive was a primary feature of World War II in contrast to World War I. With the release of the first two atomic weapons the trend rose drastically higher. It has been that way ever since—with a consequence of unprecedented degrees and an unprecedented range of anxiety in international affairs. Until and unless some way of redressing the imbalance—enabling defensive power to shorten the gap—is achieved, the easier sort of relative stability experienced in past epochs will remain beyond reach. Each side in the great confrontation is aware of possibilities of reaping great advantage by being first to develop techniques for nullifying the other side's offensive power while holding on to its own absolute offensive capability. Each side must also be aware of the vital importance of keeping up with the other in this respect and of finding ways figuratively to flank any temporarily efficacious defensive technique developed by the opponent.

Meanwhile, the pre-eminent adversaries in the competition have to rely primarily on weapons intrinsically unsuitable to defensive operations in that they can only be turned against an adversary's homeland and are of no use for intercepting attack—in contrast to the double capabilities for attacking and for warding off attack generally characteristic of weaponry in other epochs. Neither side can feel confident of escaping ruinous damage. Each relies for security on inculcating a like consciousness in the other. I wish neither to deplore nor to celebrate these factors but only to trace their unfolding effects on the Atlantic Alliance.

The assumption initially reflected in Alliance strategy was to prove highly impermanent. Two fairly close occurrences overturned them. The first was the Soviet Union's achievement of capability in atomic fission in the latter part of 1949, considerably ahead of the time anticipated on this side. The second was the launching of an attack southward across the 38th parallel against the Republic of Korea in June of 1950—a portentous occurrence following by less than a year the notable aggrandizement of Communist dominion in the winning of mainland China. The Soviet atomic achievement brought into close prospect an end to the United States' monopoly of prodigious weapons and opened a prospect, moreover, of early Soviet progress in weaponry of hugely greater potential, namely the hydrogen weapon. The implications of the second event seem less certain in retrospect—a point worth a moment's consideration.

Unequivocal advance assurances of protection had not been given South Korea. Accordingly, some would emphasize, Communist willingness to use force in testing for opportunity to establish dominion over that area and to reunite Korea under Communist aegis did not necessarily betoken a disposition to defy protective guarantees respecting other regions. According to this line of argument, the United States reacted excessively to the challenge in Korea, and the drastic responses undertaken with respect to Atlantic defenses were uncalled for. The argument is not convincing, and hindsight is not always a better judge than the insight of a crucial moment. The potential for erosion of confidence in Europe in the wake of the attack in Korea seemed enormous and menacing, though its actuality and extent would have been verifiable only under conditions of a failure to take compensatory measures. I venture —and no one is entitled to a more assertive verb with respect to a question of what would have happened if the things that really happened had not happened—that if a stand had not been made in Korea, a sharp, and perhaps determinative, turn for the worse in the Atlantic framework would have been unavoidable.

The Korean War provided an occasion and a stimulus, but the need for revaluation and revision of strategy was derived from now manifest Soviet progress in the nuclear field, for under contemporary conditions a sudden advance in invention tends to reverberate in the same way a seizure of strategic territory did in past epochs. As custodian of the strategic anchor, the United States decided to press on with development of a still more prodigious weapon array in the hydrogen fusion bomb and with improvements in delivery systems and in techniques for early warning of attacks directed against the American position, lest determinative advantages should fall to the Soviet Union. Within the framework of the Alliance proper a number of important steps were proposed, with variant results.

One step was establishment of a supreme and engrossing military command structure to provide the Alliance greater coherence in plans and operations. This was done. A second step was inclusion of Greece and Turkey, so as to add important positions and manpower resources and to give the Alliance scope on the southern flank through the eastern Mediterranean. This was done. A third step concerned deployment of sizable American conventional forces in Europe to serve as an increment of posted strength, to encourage the European participants to marshal will for greater effort, and, most importantly, to provide hostages as an earnest, to adversary and allies, of the absoluteness of the American commitment to European security. This was done. Fourth was conversion of occupied West Germany into a participant in the Alliance and its councils as a military resource rather than a liability. This, too, was done, finally, after long and futile dalliance with the intricate concept of a supranational European army under conditions subordinating German forces to Alliance command and foreclosing Germany from manufacture of a range of sensitive weapons, including nuclear weapons. The fifth step involved increases in military contributions to the Alliance by the other European principals. This was debated, resolved about, hedged, and, in final analysis, not really done. The propensity of togetherness for promoting big talk is well known. Collective frameworks almost invariably tempt governments into declaratory intentions far in excess of their wills to perform. With respect to this last item, the Alliance proved no exception.

A third phase in Alliance history opened with a decision in 1954 to substitute tactical nuclear weapons—under United States possession and control—for increments of manpower at the European bulwarks, a development logically in keeping with a concurrent phase in American military policy of preoccupation with trying to load missions onto prodigious weaponry, a phase identified by such phrases as "the new look" and "more bang for a buck."

The next phase is, broadly speaking, one still in progress in 1964. The technical developments bringing it about were cumulative. Soviet achievement of hydrogen weapons was revealed as early as 1953—even a little ahead of the United States. Conjecturally, the realization of this capability was accompanied by advances in bomber developments adding a portion of danger for the United States. Dire portents of the trend, however, rose signally in men's consciousness after the launching of Sputnik in 1957, with

its corollary implication of missile systems capable of vault-
ing warning networks and outracing interception. Strategically, in this phase the United States has been brought unequivocally within the target area. This circumstance affords
considerable potential leverage to the adversary. Theo-
retically, in event of full-scale war, the Soviet Union would
have an option between directing its attack on the United
States while sparing Europe or vice versa. Thereby a considerable doubt is engendered, a doubt repeatedly denied
and allayed but still persistent in many minds.

The United States' current emphasis is on laying a basis
for plausible conduct of hostilities in event of war. This
calls for non-nuclear strength sufficient to make a contest,
at least for a while, in event of an attack in kind; a reserve
of tactical nuclear weapons to enable our side to raise
combat to that level if necessary; a strategic array of nuclear strength capable of gravely and decisively impairing
the adversary's retaliatory nuclear capability in event of our
being forced to take initiative in that kind of strategic war;
and, finally, a further nuclear capability to inhibit adversary
nuclear initiatives through its power to inflict unacceptable retaliatory damage. This strategy would make Central and Western Europe, in extremity, an area to be fought
over—a dour prospect for peoples and governments of the
area.

One must refer back to the 1954 decision—prompted by
frugality rather than strategic theory—to deploy tactical
nuclear weapons to Europe. Men are impelled to bridge,
one way or another, between theory and practice. By the
concept eventually fashioned in this instance, the big thing
was not to fight a war rationally, in event of having to
fight one at all, but to forestall war altogether, an aim to
be served more convincingly by nuclear weapons for the
battlefield, with an implicit threat of immediately having
to raise the level of combat to prodigious heights, than by
an increment of men and weapons of lower potential. By

an opposite argument, a prospect of having to go at once to such drastic and unknowledgeable lengths of destruction might more readily paralyze one's own resolve than deter a challenger. Whatever the merits, the former line of hypothesis has taken firm hold among the European allies. Their preference is for a strategy to obviate even a small calculable probability of ever having to be employed: a strategy involving high probability of an early nuclear exchange in event of hostilities and, as an implicit corollary, a high probability of making the United States, in dire event, the adversary's prime target.

Whether the United States would honor its commitments is a question basic to the North Atlantic Alliance, for any answer short of a firm affirmative would fail of the necessary degree of deterrence to the adversary and of assurance to partners. The United States' six divisions remain in West Germany as a concrete guarantee supporting the pledge of involvement in event of attack from the East. Their presence crowds the restricted maneuver areas of West Germany, so that the latter government must shop around in France, Spain, and even Scotland for room to train its soldiery. It reflects no military necessity, for troops of equivalent number would be readily enough deployable to scenes of action in extremity. The United States' forces are there to foreclose any presumption of a possibility of default. The U.S. is at a loss as to how to withdraw or even substantially to reduce them without weakening that assurance. Yet their presence seems to inhibit additions of conventional strength among European participants fearful of hastening the day of withdrawal— and thereby precipitating a detraction from the assurance — by providing substitute forces.

The United States' commitment remains pre-eminent as a factor in the military efficacy of the Alliance. The deployment of forces to substantiate warnings against transgression is in one direction—from west to east—across the

Atlantic, and the nuclear resources essential to sustain the defenses are under United States ownership and control. The arrangements are inherently asymmetrical, with the United States, as from the beginning, in the role of main and essential determiner of Alliance strategy. This special role, with its related prerogatives and burdens, has been a source of recurring tensions within the Alliance, but the issues have not impinged upon the integrity of the strategic structure. Whatever its unresolved differences, the Alliance has worked and continues to work as a military undertaking. The continuous exercise in notional warfare has sustained the allies' confidence; the unremitting query as to the probable character and course of hypothetical war, on a basis of factors presumably apparent to the adversary, has brought an assuring answer of the improbability of real war.

Because of its inherent preventive character, one cannot prove the effects of the Alliance. We shall never be able to ascertain, but can only conjecture, the course of events that would have obtained in the absence of such an Alliance. How far the compact may have stayed adversary purposes, what desperate straits may have been averted, are questions susceptible of no proof. The past does not reveal its alternatives. This observation bears on a recurrent fallacy, which I have sometimes heard in high places. By this fallacy, dire possibilities which one has anticipated and taken pains to ward off and which thereupon failed to materialize were never really in the cards anyway—like counting the hire of a watchman as needless because, in all his time on the job, no thief has come in the night.

The Lingering Problem of Accommodation with the Adversary

Unlike history, policy does not subsist on the past. Whatever its accomplishments up to now in marshaling force to forefend against war and its intimidatory shadow, the Alliance is troubled and its future clouded. Doubts and difficulties pertain both to defining conditions for a settled, legitimate order in succession to the menacing confrontation which gave rise to the Alliance and to determining the frame of authority for defining those conditions. These problems, involving questions of value and the locus of decision and falling, therefore, in the catchall category called political, have a bearing on the future cogency of the Alliance as a military undertaking.

The factors of difference between the obvious successes and the apparent frustrations in the Alliance's record pertain, in an elementary way, to the degree of the Alliance's autonomy with respect to problems concerned and, conversely, to the degree and character of response required from the Communist side.

Even the minimal aim of forefending against war and related intimidatory gestures is contingent, obviously, on decisions and actions taken on the Communist side. Reluctant or otherwise, Communist compliance in desisting from the launching of force is a condition necessary to success. The power of decision in supplying means of insuring this compliance, however, in so far as marshaling of force and manifestation of will can serve to ensure it, lies with the Alliance members.

The Alliance enjoys no such autonomy with respect to achieving peace, conceived as a pervasive and reliable legitimate order. Settled arrangements reflecting reciprocal confidence and assent would be necessary constituents of success in this purpose. Such arrangements would have to be contractual in form and spirit. Explicit mutual steps would have to be negotiated. The course would be contingent upon Communist—specifically Soviet —intentions in every phase.

The idea of coming to terms with the Soviet adversary over relevant issues of dominion, jurisdiction, and security respecting Europe, far from having been neglected, has been a focus of diplomatic interchanges of unmatched thoroughness and persistence dating back to World War II. The protracted exercises have got no closer to substance than exploring possibilities of negotiating about points of substance, with each side testing notional alternatives to the confrontation, without as yet achieving agreement. Concerning conceptual possibilities for settlement, as distinguished from calculable probabilities, the redundant negotiations about negotiating have only confirmed in experience what should be inferrable by logic.

The possibilities—four in number, two of them with one side prevailing and the other giving in, and the other two reflecting stalemate—are: retraction of Soviet power in acquiescence to the Alliance and to the United States' interposition in Europe; withdrawal of United States power and thus liquidation of the Alliance with Soviet sway left undiminished; reciprocal retraction of United States and Soviet power; and indefinite continuation of present alignments with both sides reconciled and assured of reciprocity.

Deliberately designed and documented changes are not the only ones possible. The pattern, as I am aware, might be changed by unraveling as well as through planned intention. Here, however, discussion is focused on the idea of coming to terms—not that of losing control. The aim is to examine the entailments for a settled order encompassing Europe and to examine, as well, how these entailments bear on problems confronting the Alliance.

Whatever their content, such arrangements, if validly realized, would signify conditions amounting to a renewal of the Concert of Europe in some form. The conditions would presumably be susceptible of being extended from Europe, as a base, to the world in general and would provide, at least in concept, a workable foundation for a collective security system as predicated in the Charter. As a postulate—one can scarcely assert it as a fact—arrangements settled on in Europe would be reflected globally. Retraction of Soviet power accompanied by Soviet acquiescence in United States interposition in Europe would indicate a Soviet disposition to accommodate everywhere. Unilateral United States withdrawal from the confrontation, leaving the adversary position intact, would signal a disposition to knuckle under in general. Reciprocal retraction of United States and Soviet power from the European arena would signify an easing of opposed purposes in other theaters. Mutual reconciliation along present lines would similarly project as a sort of tired standoff elsewhere.

Beyond a purpose to avoid an outcome leaving Soviet power intact and triumphant in Europe, and beyond what may be construed from the twenty-year span of obligation, the treaty gives no clues to the character, timing, and other circumstances of the hoped-for easement. Whether the Alliance should continue in effect afterwards or be phased out as a condition thereto—a matter obviously beyond the Alliance members' autonomous power to ordain—is not specified. Hope is pinned on nothing more definite than promoting—to borrow George Kennan's phrase— "tendencies which must eventually find their outlets in either the break-up or the gradual mellowing of Soviet power."[8]

The advent of the Eisenhower Administration produced, besides the military modification noted, an attempt to bring about a more specific political focus, with *liberation* the watchword and Secretary of State John Foster Dulles the articulator:

> What we need to do is recapture to some extent the kind of crusading spirit of the early days when we were darn sure that what we had was a lot better than what anybody else had. We knew the rest of the world

---

[8] George F. Kennan, *American Diplomacy, 1900–1950* (Chicago: University of Chicago Press, 1951), p. 127.

wanted it, and needed it, and that we were going to
carry it around the world. . . .[9]

Soviet power would retreat. As to means of compelling
this outcome, "Those who don't believe results can be
achieved by moral pressure, by the weight of propaganda,
don't know what they are talking about," Mr. Dulles told
senators at his pre-confirmation hearing.[10] Less than four
years later, the United States and its allies, short of will
and appropriate capabilities, stood by during the episode
of Hungary and drew consolation from moral condem-
nations and an exercise known as mobilizing forces of world
opinion, and the season closed on the Dulles prescription
for liberation.

Attempts at settlement and accommodation, however,
were not foreclosed by the verbal devotion to a liberation
strategy characteristic of the Eisenhower tenure. These
were pursued in a series of ministerial meetings, produced
one tangible result in the Austrian State Treaty, and engendered two seasons of general, superficial promise in
connection with direct encounters at the supreme level of
authority at Geneva in 1955 and then at Camp David in
1959. Prospects glowed in discussions focused on generalities of peace and good intention but faded at contact
with specifics. The contradictions of parleying about peace
while prosecuting opposed purposes set the stage for a
grand anticlimax, at Paris in the spring of 1960, involving
a Soviet Prime Minister in dudgeon, an American President in wordless distress, a British Prime Minister in tears,
a French President in preoccupied contemplation, and all

[9] John Robinson Beal, *John Foster Dulles* (New York: Harper, 1957),
p. 310.
[10] *Nomination of John Foster Dulles, Secretary of State—Designate,
Hearings Before the Committee on Foreign Relations, United States
Senate, 83rd Congress, First Session* (Washington: Government Printing
Office, 1953), p. 6.

four in predicament. The quest was suspended thereupon to await a changeover in Washington.

Achievements, officially asserted, from the resumption and reinvigoration of efforts toward accommodation during subsequent years include installation of a Moscow-Washington teletype link for quick communication in dire emergency, a nuclear test-ban treaty, agreement in principle on law for outer space, joint acceptance of a United Nations' resolution banning weapons in orbit, suspension of Soviet jamming of the Voice of America, a transaction for sales of wheat to the Soviet Union, and concurrent decisions by the two governments for proportionate reductions in production of uranium and plutonium for nuclear weapons—with additional progress claimed in negotiations toward a consular convention and a new cultural exchange program.[11] One's appraisal of the extrinsic significance of such a list is likely to turn on one's inclination as between interpreting events in light of hopes and construing expectations by measuring events.

The test-ban treaty serves as an example of relevant ambiguity. By it, in Senator Fulbright's hopeful interpretation, "each side in effect assured the other that it was prepared to forego, at least for the present, any bid for a decisive military or political breakthrough."[12] A contrasting interpretation would stress the perseverance on each side in testing to a point of marginal utility before the shutdown. It would stress the failure to include in the agreement the one environment requiring on-site inspection as a means of verification and involving, therefore, a point of difference basic to issues in the confrontation with the Soviet union. Such an interpretation would emphasize, also, the inclusion of terms for abrogation of the agreement at the convenience and discretion of the parties—something like a marriage

[11] *Washington Post and Times-Herald,* January 3 and April 21, 1964; Press Release No. 328, American Embassy, Bonn, February 18, 1964.

[12] *New York Times,* March 26, 1964.

contract with a protocol for divorce—a point justifying a purist in regarding the undertaking as a treaty only in name.

So it goes with the other items. Equipment for instant communication does not affect substance to be communicated. Agreement on law for outer space is marginal to agreement on legitimacy in Europe and over the globe itself. An orbital-weapon ban forecloses something not yet known to be feasible and probably redundant strategically. The Voice of America permitted to be heard, for the time being, is bland. The wheat deal mainly serves, at a subsidized price, to succor the Soviet Union from consequences of improvident policies and has no impact whatever on the Soviet Union's use of exterior trade as an instrument of politics and strategy. The announced reductions in uranium and plutonium increments are like swearing off on third helpings of ice cream. I should concur with Hans Morgenthau's estimate: "None of these . . . changes has any bearing on the substance of the cold war, while only one of them bears upon its modalities, and in a way . . . detrimental to the interests of the United States."[13]

Official discourse concedes the smallness of the steps taken, but alleges great portent: "Small steps . . . worth taking because we may find them to be the key to larger ones," according to the Secretary of State.[14] Thus—to quote Morgenthau again—does policy "search for the swallow which will make a summer." The assumptions and attitudes reflected in the pressing of negotiations are ones long established in the American approach to world affairs: a habit of extolling peace in tones of invoking policy, a postulate of basic harmony of interest among all nations derived from a common stock of reason, and faith in transforming issues by talking them over—a concept of an in-

---

[13] Hans Morgenthau, "Peace in Our Time?," *Commentary*, March, 1964, p. 67.

[14] *Washington Post and Times-Herald*, January 3, 1964.

herent efficacy of negotiation as an avenue for finding agreement. The mystique of negotiation has been summed up by a spokesman for United States foreign policy:

> The essence of a normal business transaction is that each party, from his own point of view, makes a gain. There is no reason why, with proper caution and much patience, we cannot arrive at agreement of this kind with the Soviet Union.[15]

The hope in which such attitudes converge is that of achieving détente. Circumstances abetting such hope include the current style of Soviet discourse under Premier Nikita Khrushchev's spokesmanship, deepening cleavage between the Soviet Union and China, and cumulation of nuclear striking power in American and Soviet possession. Brief elaboration and analysis of each of these circumstances is fitting.

Notwithstanding George Kennan's appeal to Americans not to be "put off by the angularities of Mr. Khrushchev's personality,"[16] the subject personage's peasant rotundity gives an essentially subtle operator an advantage of not appearing subtle at all. An item in the Khrushchev armory is his custom of parading every purpose, however inimical, as peaceable. His success in winning wide acceptance, as a synonym for accommodation, of his favored formulation of the Soviet version for peace—peaceful coexistence—epitomizes his accomplishment in attracting attention to the block letters, and away from the fine print, of Soviet intentions. Remarks by the Secretary of State, in a dour phase of his alternation between somber and bright outlooks on world affairs, put a proper measure on the protestations of peaceful purpose:

---

[15] Press Release No. 328, Embassy of the United States, Bonn, February 18, 1964.

[16] George F. Kennan, *Russia and the West Under Lenin and Stalin* (Boston: Little, Brown, 1961), p. 394.

No one has to convince us that when Khrushchev said communism will bury us he was proclaiming not just an alleged historic inevitability but an objective toward which Communists work relentlessly by all means they deem effective. No one has to convince us that peaceful coexistence means to them a continuing attempt to spread their system over the earth by all means short of the great war that would be self-defeating. No one has to convince us that the contest . . . is for keeps.[17]

The quarrel between Moscow and Peking is rated as a windfall in coping with Communist power—a factor to temper Soviet intransigence if not convert the adversary to amicability for all practical purposes. In a manner recently exemplified by the Secretary of State, these assumptions may be projected to taking sides, more or less, with Moscow in its rivalry with Peking.[18] I should accept Morgenthau's summation: "The issue . . . is in the short run the leadership of world communism; in the long run it is the same issue that currently divides the United States and the Soviet Union: who shall inherit the earth?" [19] The proposition that *ipso facto* one's enemy's enemy is a friend of sorts led to great fallacies of policy in World War II and is little likely to serve us better now. In choosing among opponents so disposed, relative armed potential is a criterion as plausible, to say the least, as militance· of current tone. Whatever opportunity may be offered by division within the Communist camp could be exploited against the stronger element as plausibly— here I understate purposely—as against the one more wayward for the time being.

In commonplaces of the time, the potency for destruction represented in nuclear striking power divided between

[17] *Department of State Bulletin*, September 3, 1962, p. 343.

[18] *Washington Post and Times-Herald*, December 17, 1963.

[19] Morgenthau, "Peace in Our Time?" p. 67.

American and Soviet possession has rendered war impossible and unthinkable and peace inevitable, nuclear weapons useless for supporting sensible policy, and the idea of winning has been rendered obsolete. I am often at a loss whether to concur in such propositions before knowing whether they are offered as mental shorthand or as conclusive concepts. Though using them myself, I question some of the significances attributed to them. Shared belief in high probability of war under calculable circumstances, which the respective sides are loath to bring about, underlies current strategic stability. The high probability of avoiding a contest at arms stems from the thinking done about war—a prudential consideration, not something inherent. Notwithstanding the often declared impossibility of using nuclear arms to support sensible policy, capacity to use them and the companion possibility can serve a sensible policy. War is avoided by generating knowledge of its imminent potential. Peace persists through attentive effort growing out of recognition of its tenuousness. Such peace as is realized represents scant concord beyond a shared desire to avoid hostilities—an agreement not produced by negotiation. The cliché about the obsoleteness of winning is easily tested. The term in question is not necessarily absolute. It may stand for making headway with one's purposes—maintaining them as valid and solvent—in face of what opposes them. Events have not superseded the idea of winning, and they will not supersede it until, in some unimaginable circumstance, the opposite possibility, losing, has been eliminated.

The workings, rather than the intrinsic validity, of the notions dealt with concern us here. The analogues to ideas shaping policy in World War II and its immediate aftermath are obvious. Khrushchev's style serves to renew and to reinforce belief in general reasonableness and belief in fundamental mutuality of interests underlying the moment's differences and bound to emerge and to transform issues—

given patience and plenty of talk. The hopes for world concord in the mid-40's were based on such beliefs. China, in the role of common adversary, is considered a sort of substitute for the Axis foemen of World War II, in providing cement for entente with the Soviet Union. Shared comprehension of nuclear lethality as something bigger than both of us—a danger transcendent over conflicts of values and interests related to ideology—is viewed as a solvent equivalent to what was supposed to be provided by experiences of battle in the hopes of 1945. Bonds of understanding and shared responsibility are projected as emerging realities, if not yet full-blown. They become predicates supporting an aspiration to vindicate the dream, never really put aside, of structuring world peace on a basis of general concord—a motif objectified in the Charter. In hopeful imagination, the idea of détente leads on to an entente with the Soviet Union as a counterpoise and eventually a successor to the Alliance. In effect, a framework of assumptions expressible as the Yalta pattern emerges.

Such is the aura of détente—something felt to be under way if not yet in sight of fulfillment. In one perspective, the reality of such a process as détente inheres in the assumptions of entities concerned. Views of a determining number in determining positions are determining. A change in frames of mind among those dealing with great affairs, even though a matter of imagination, rates as a change of reality, for attitudes are part of reality in foreign affairs. Yet the very subjectivity of the word puts in question any attempt at prediction. The moment's anticipation may mark a start of an enduring trend or prove as insubstantial as the nimbus of Geneva and Camp David in 1955 and 1959, when urge for accommodation boggled on specific terms. Discussion thus brings us to consideration of the price of a détente now, to its relation to the future

of the Alliance, and its connection with the questions sha-
dowing it.

The Prospects and the Price of Accommodation

Finding the Soviet Union amenable to bargaining in the
mode of what a United States spokesman has described as
a "normal business transaction," which enables each party
to make a gain from its own point of view, is a reasonably
adequate expression of favorable conditions for the Alliance as a design for a situation of strength, on the basis
of which a settlement could be attempted.

From adversary relationships in international affairs
to normal business dealing is a large leap—one not to be
accomplished merely by verbalizing. Of itself, the cited
assertion of "no reason why, with proper caution and much
patience, we cannot arrive at agreements of this kind" does
not bridge the gap. The past has shown manifold reasons.
They are not susceptible of being overridden by declaration.
As a central point of difficulty in the past, the purpose of
the other side in the bargaining attempts has been to
eliminate the basis from which to approach bargaining on
this side. By logic, the likelihood of finding opportunity
for significant mutual gains in such a circumstance is
ruled out. The analogy to "normal business transaction"
is inapplicable. A more apt analogue would be that of a
trading relationship between a gunsmith and a customer
imbued with intentions of subsequently holding up the gunsmith.

So far, the idea of negotiating a way to settlement in
Europe—however attractive to American preferences and
expectations—has repeatedly stranded on the circumstance of incompatible purposes. Yet hope of somehow
talking a way to agreement has persisted. The simple logical difficulty of squaring hope with circumstance comes

through clearly in a pronouncement by the Secretary of State: the Soviet Union's implacable hostility of intention is postulated; our policies are conceived as a formula for enabling everybody to come out ahead and specifically pointed toward mutually advantageous permanent solutions in Central Europe.[20] The hopeful good will in that formulation is unchallengeable. Doubts pertain only to logic. The effect is like multiplying a negative and a positive number and getting a positive result. Something is missing from the equation. The ideas do not fit into syllogisms. From a frame of logic, they dangle like the notion of solving large central problems by attending to small marginal ones.

One may find a supposititious way out of the difficulty by predicating conversion of the adversary. I should not presume to rule out all possibility of a transformation of outlook and conviction by action of some moral equivalent of a seizure along the road to Damascus.

The question is one of evidence not of explanation of logical possibilities. A change in manner is apparent—even a change of method—but so far not one prudently to be construed as a reform of purpose. Events in Cuba, Cyprus, Yemen, and so on indicate an adversary more deft but no less inimical and resolute than in the past. In my estimate, notions of a transformed adversary reflect wish rather than reality. That is not to gainsay a real significance of heightened expectations for détente, measured in effects on the Alliance.

However simple in its logical essences, the problem imposed by the double task which the United States has been essaying—maintaining the Alliance intact, or even improving it, and simultaneously seeking détente—is difficult in practical terms. The purposes tend to come into contradiction. The reason for having combined lies in the out-

---

[20] *Department of State Bulletin, loc. cit.*

sider's hostile intractability. To render him amicable and
tractable removes the reason for combining. Lapse of motivation for combining relieves pressure on him to be
tractable. In this sense, an alliance conceived in strictly
defensive terms is inherently subject to manipulation.
The reactivity may approach that of Sweet Alice in the
song, "who wept with delight when you gave her a smile,
and trembled with fear at your frown."

Such an alliance, moreover, is likely to be far more
unified on reasons for resisting than on terms for accommodating. The locus of authority in judging the relevant
considerations and in arriving at terms, whether conceived
as those of détente or more definitively as a settlement,
involves great potential issues. Their imminence and significance grow in proportion to the emphasis and energy
brought to bear in seeking to negotiate an easement, and
in proportion to the degree of likelihood accorded the prospect of success.

From a determining position in Alliance strategy, as
custodian of the nuclear underpinning, the United States
is projected into pre-eminence in quest of satisfactory permanent arrangements with the Soviet Union, and, indeed, a
desire to prevent diffusion of that prerogative with respect
to hopes of negotiating for arms control with the Soviet
Union and of approaching a European settlement is not
least among reasons for seeking to restrain the proliferation of nuclear weapons, and it is also part of the rationale behind the nuclear test-ban treaty. The principals
in the nuclear cartel, reflecting a strategic equilibrium con-
sonant with nuclear stalemate, are seen as arbiters over
the future of Europe. Mutuality of understanding, assumed
to be operative between the nuclear principals, takes on a
character of entente. Bonds of collaboration between them
are given increasing emphasis.

Ipso facto—notwithstanding the declaratory aim of holding onto and even strengthening the Alliance while pushing

initiatives for easement with the adversary—considerations integral to the Alliance framework are concomitantly downgraded. The Alliance texture is affected adversely. Here it is in point to trace some of the effects with respect to allies across the Atlantic—the main ones in the central range of the Alliance, namely the United Kingdom, France, and the German Federal Republic.

The first instance presents no trouble. By reason of a modest auxiliary portion of nuclear capability that was undertaken in 1954 during the phase of Alliance strategy which emphasized such weaponry for tactical uses, the United Kingdom shares in the nuclear cartel as a minor member. Moreover, on the merits of détente, the United Kingdom is so thoroughly at one with the United States as to make it unnecessary to decide which one to cast as the Don and which as the ever faithful squire in the quixotic quest.

With respect to the two continental allies mentioned, the prospect summons up remembrance. A shift of emphasis for the United States from its role of principal deterrer to that of principal bargainer in the effort to arrive at conditions for the future of Europe with the Soviet Union suggests sensitive parallels to the Yalta phase. The situation of each country is vastly different now in comparison both to that phase and to the circumstances obtaining upon entry into the Alliance. Each has experienced a recovery, in part with United States subvention. Each has undergone a transforming experience politically—France under President Charles de Gaulle's endeavor to reintegrate public life and national authority, and the German Federal Republic in being taken into the councils of the Alliance and converted from ex-enemy to ally status. Neither, obviously, has forgotten its time in eclipse—the one as a beaten ally reduced to client status and the other as a defeated enemy at the conqueror's disposal.

As to France's case, the impulsions are complex. One

must take care not to misstate the matter and not to exaggerate the argument. From the standpoint of the United States' preferences, France's attitude in the Alliance appears wayward. Client status is recalled as humiliation, especially by President de Gaulle. The United Kingdom's reputed special relationship to the United States dates back to the same period. President de Gaulle recalls a vain bid, broached in 1958, to share that special relationship on a basis of parity, thus to set up a triune directorate for the Alliance.[21] His program for restoring France's importance in world affairs centers on capability in manufacture and delivery of nuclear weapons. The explicit purpose is to gain for France a franchise in nuclear matters at least equivalent to that disposed by the United Kingdom and thereby a higher rating in the striking of bargains, one to insure being listened to and to avoid being overridden or ignored.

France's avowed justification rests on doubts of the United States' constancy with respect to commitments to defend Europe. Prospects of having nuclear capability come into hands of an ally disposed to work at crosspurposes raise dire possibilities. In imaginable extremity, United States forces in Europe might become hostages to a dissentient ally's pressure. Continuation of the deployment in that circumstance would come into some question. Withdrawal of the forces would undercut the Alliance's credibility and vindicate French doubts. To that extent, France's course tends to induce the circumstance

---

[21] The character of President de Gaulle's bid has been elucidated by James Reston in the following words: "In his private memorandum to President Eisenhower of Sept. 17, 1958, de Gaulle said that there must be a United States-French-British organization to take *joint* decisions on questions affecting Western strategy anywhere in the world, and specifically decisions on any use of nuclear weapons. In short, a French and British veto on the use of American nuclear power unless the United States were attacked." *The New York Times,* May 3, 1964.

claimed in justification and exploits protection afforded by the Alliance to ends unfavorable to that protection.

The aim here is not to settle the merits of France's course but to trace the relevance of questions raised by the quest for détente—as to which, incidentally, the French government's estimates of probabilities have been as shifting and ambiguous as the American. An assumption of the adversary's imminent amenability to a measure of accommodation that would be compatible with the Alliance's integrity and purposes signally reduces the seriousness of the implications of France's bid to cut in on the nuclear cartel. Moreover, by that assumption, France's desire for nuclear credentials for entry into the bargaining circle becomes quite comprehensible. On the other hand, one may assume, as I do, the delusiveness of the idea of an adversary at last, or on the verge of being, converted to tractability. That premise puts the United States' judgment of realities into question and makes comprehensible an ally's desire to hedge its position. In sum, the reprehensibility of France's course is inverse to belief in Soviet tractability, and it is contradictory to reprove France and to court the adversary.

Simpler but also more serious and central questions rise with respect to the German Federal Republic. Though in many ways the most successful of the European participants, and among them, the source of the greatest contribution of military strength to the Alliance, the German Federal Republic bears awareness of being incomplete—a truncated portion of the country, with the eastern portion of the land under Soviet domination and the western portion in position neither to acquiesce in, nor to overturn, the fact. As in the beginning of the confrontation, Germany remains the focal point of issues over the future of Europe—the locality for testing whether the idea of a reservoir of opportunities for working out mutual gains with the Soviet Union represents actuality or is diplomatic happy talk; a testing ground also for the concept, fascinating to United States foreign policy, of persevering in negotiation of small and marginal issues in expectation of thereby transforming large and central ones.

In relation to Germany, one can best understand the dilemmas posed by pursuit of détente. The German instance brings one to the bare bones of logical possibilities for settlement in Europe—Soviet retraction, leaving the Alliance triumphant; United States retraction, leaving the Soviet Union encamped; reciprocal retraction by interpositions by both sides; and reciprocal acquiescence in existing lines, legitimizing zones of authority and influence as they are.

Détente means the last—a point not to be concealed by verbal distinctions between *de facto* and *de jure* and so on. Détente means a bargain by the paramount powers, the principals of the nuclear cartel, over the sharing of Germany. The Yalta prototype rises, with implications of acute sensitivity. In being bargained over in a settlement between the paramount powers, Germany's status would descend implicitly to that of an ex-enemy country again. The Soviet Union, moreover, would be shown to hold the keys to Germany's future. Alienation of the Federal Republic from the Alliance would presumably follow in natural course. The Alliance would be hurt as a going concern. The flow of events would tend toward the second of the possibilities listed.

Yet for the Federal Republic to be associated as an ally in a decision disposing the future of Germany as a whole is logically and practically incompatible with terms likely to be conceded by the Soviet Union in circumstances short of a determinative defeat of its purposes in Central Europe.

With respect to Germany, one sees how soon the course of détente comes to dead end—how soon exploration for possibilities of mutual gain must play out. Within the limitations, it may well be prudent to negotiate on small matters for their intrinsic worth, however slight, but only harm is likely to result from avowing expansive importance for the effort. Such avowal implies basic misunderstanding of the problems of dealing with the adversary, puts to doubt the United States' grasp of the requirements, and thereby, is all too likely to derogate from the credibility of the Alliance.[22]

The unpromising character of available avenues to settlement brings one back to consideration of an indefinite prolongation of confrontation, to acceptance of what President Kennedy in his inaugural address called "a hard and bitter peace," as the best in sight even with its tensions. This would be a morally taxing course, for "hope long deferred maketh the heart sick." The Alliance as a whole would have to remain indefinitely content with, or at least devoted to, its proximate goals. This prospect poses a question with respect to every member of the Alliance, but especially with respect to the German Federal Republic,

---

[22] A report—at hand as I write—of an interview given by President Johnson to the weekly *Quick,* of Munich, points up the difficulty of applying to the actual situation the abstractions associated with the mood of détente. See *Ibid.,* April 29, 1964. The gist is to "put yourself in the place of the Russians," to "try to understand their feelings," to "allay their concerns," and to seek "better relations" with the Soviet Union. By definition, each of the ideas has appeal. Empathy is preferable to alienation. Understanding is preferable to miscomprehension. Alleviation sounds better than aggravation. Yet the focus of issues between the Soviet Union and the Federal Republic of Germany is the fact of the latter government's having turned westward in developing political associations, having entered the Atlantic Alliance, and not having acquiesced to the proposition of the rightfulness of the Soviet-supported German Democratic Republic. Better relations, judged from the Soviet Union's standpoint, would involve reversal of those positions. Improving relations in that direction would correlate to worsening relations with the Federal Republic's allies, including the United States. Implicit in the interview is an idea of an underlying harmony of interest regarding Germany as between the United States and the other Western allies on one hand and the Soviet Union on the other. As the central essence of the German problem, these respective interests are opposed.

where pressures to seek terms on its own with the Soviet Union regarding Germany's future as a whole would presumably become increasingly formidable. Not a prepossessing prospect, I repeat, but those disposed to reject it should come up with a plausible case for something better.

The Sino-Soviet Dispute and the West: The Soviet Aspect

by
*Richard Lowenthal**

How serious are the differences on policy toward the West underlying the Sino-Soviet dispute? How far has Chinese pressure, exerted in the framework of that dispute, influenced Soviet policy toward the West and how far is it likely to do so in the future? What long-range effects on Soviet policy toward the West are likely to flow from the open ideological schism between Soviet and Chinese communism? What could or should the West do to influence the course of the conflict?

This set of questions, or at least part of them, has formed the subject of discussion among Western analysts ever since the first indications of serious policy disagreements between Moscow and Peking appeared in 1958–59; and

* *Richard Lowenthal:* Born and educated in Germany, went to Britain during the Hitler years. Holds the chair of international relations at the Free University of West Berlin. His book on *World Communism: The Disintegration of a Secular Faith* will be published in English this year.

as the dispute increased in scope and intensity, so did the debate on its relevance for the West. The following remarks can attempt no more than to present briefly the author's viewpoint in this debate, in the light of the facts that have become available at the time of writing.

I

The scope of Sino-Soviet differences on policy toward the West, though important in itself, has been persistently exaggerated by the polemical distortions with which each side presented the views of the other. The Soviets have misrepresented the Chinese as regarding nuclear world war as inevitable or even desirable; the Chinese have misrepresented the Soviets as willing to renounce all use of force against the "imperialists," and particularly all support for revolutionary "liberation movements," for the sake of peaceful coexistence and to reduce the entire struggle against the "imperialist camp" to peaceful economic competition. For a realistic appraisal, it is essential to judge the policy of either side by its own statements and actions, not by the statements of the other.

Such an examination of the record shows that the Soviet and Chinese Communists have based their different policies throughout on the same traditional, Leninist principles. Both believed and still believe that the world-wide advance of the Communist cause must be fostered by a combination of violent and peaceful, of revolutionary and diplomatic, means; both are also in agreement that a nuclear world war between the "socialist" and "imperialist" camps can and should be avoided. The Chinese have emphasized that wars are inevitable while imperialism exists, but have never made such a statement with regard to nuclear world war—nor have they denied that diplomatic negotiation with the enemy, including "summit meetings," may form a useful part of the struggle against imperialism.[1] The Soviets have stressed the dangers of nuclear world war and the risk of local wars escalating into world war but have explicitly stated that revolutionary "wars of liberation" and civil wars are inevitable and worthy of support.[2] Moreover, Chinese actions have fallen far short of recklessly courting a war with the United States, while Soviet actions have included the deliberate provocation of international crises by threats, among them nuclear threats, and the support of revolutionary movements by propaganda, diplomacy, and arms supplies.

The real difference, when measured in terms of statements, has often seemed merely one of emphasis. In practice, Moscow and Peking have persistently differed in their estimate of the relation of forces between the two camps and of the degree of risk to be run in any given crisis. The issue has been most truthfully stated as a contrast between a Soviet "general line" of peaceful coexistence, to which even revolutionary wars of liberation must be subordinated, and a Chinese "general line" of struggle against imperialism, to which the diplomacy of coexistence must be subordinated as one of its elements.[3]

The first moment for which these differences can be documented is the Moscow conference of Communist parties of November, 1957. Both parties were then in agreement that following the launching of the Sputniks and the implied increasing vulnerability of the U.S. to Soviet missiles, the world-wide relation of forces had shifted consid-

---

[1] For recent Chinese replies to contrary charges, see the *Red Flag* editorial "Why Does Khrushchev Spin Fabrications about 'Ruins of Destroyed Imperialism'?," *NCNA*, September 9, 1963; and the fifth joint editorial of *Red Flag* and *People's Daily*, "Two Different Lines on the Question of War and Peace," *Ibid.*, November 19, 1963.

[2] See in particular Khrushchev's report on the 1960 Moscow conference, *World Marxist Review*, January, 1961.

[3] For a fuller analysis, see R. Lowenthal, "Diplomacy and Revolution," in G. F. Hudson, R. Lowenthal, and Roderick McFarqhar, *The Sino-Soviet Dispute* (New York: Praeger, 1961).

erably in favor of the Communist camp, and that a bolder
forward policy against the West had therefore become possible than could be pursued during the post-Stalin détente
of 1953–56. But Mao's estimate of the extent of the shift
and of the chances opened by it went beyond Khrushchev's.[4] Mao's formula that "the Eastwind now prevails
over the Westwind" expressed a belief that the Communist
camp had achieved a clear superiority of strength over
its opponents; Khrushchev seems to have made the more
realistic guess that a true mutual deterrence in the nuclear
field was at last being achieved, and to have concluded
that this could be used for promoting the disintegration of
the Western Alliance by a combination of threats against
its exposed members and negotiations with the United
States, as well as for accelerating the exploitation of anticolonial movements. On this basis, Mao was concerned
that the supposed opportunities of the new world situation
should be used ruthlessly without fear of stumbling into
a nuclear war; hence, his now notorious statement about
the prospects of building "socialism" even after the annihilation of one-half of mankind.[5] The Soviets, on the other
hand, remained determined that the risk should be kept
under control even in the new situation—though they do
not seem to have reacted to Mao's statement with the same
sense of shock at the time as they manifest now: they
clearly felt that they were agreed on the main tasks, and
that owing to their own control of the decisive weapons the
difference would remain academic. The conference thus
concluded in an atmosphere of outward harmony between
Khrushchev and Mao, and it was only the Yugoslavs, de-

[4] This has been first convincingly demonstrated by A. M. Halpern,
"Communist China and Peaceful Coexistence," *China Quarterly*, No.
3, 1960.

[5] See now the Chinese government statement of September 1, 1963,
and the Soviet government statement of September 21, 1963, as issued
by *TASS* and *NCNA* respectively on these dates, for two slightly
different versions of this statement of Mao's at the 1957 conference.

feated and isolated, who carried away their horror at Mao's talk and began to spread the tale.

However, the practical import of the different Soviet and Chinese attitudes manifested itself in 1958 in the Soviet readiness to settle the mid-Eastern crisis following Kassem's coup in Iraq at a "summit meeting" in the framework of the United Nations Security Council, and again in the limitations of Soviet support for the bombardment of Quemoy. During the same year, the Soviets seem to have shown their growing anxiety about the dangers of Chinese "adventurism" by some proposal for establishing a joint naval command for the Pacific—now referred to by the Chinese as "unreasonable demands to bring China under Soviet military control" that were "rightly and firmly rejected by the Chinese government." [6] By June, 1959, the Soviets—who had still given an atomic reactor to China in September 1958—refused outright a Chinese request for a sample atomic bomb and production designs, though in the Chinese view an agreement on technological aid, concluded in October, 1957, obliged them to do so. [7] By September, 1959, the Soviets gravely offended the Chinese by taking a critical in private and, in public, a coolly neutral attitude toward their border conflict with India; [8] and the Chinese, who had not objected in principle to Khrushchev's visit to President Eisenhower, were also shocked by the manner in which Soviet propaganda proceeded to present "this imperialist chieftain" as a man of peace. When Khrushchev returned from the United States via Peking,

---

[6] First joint editorial of *Red Flag* and *People's Daily*, "The Origin and Development of the Differences between the Leadership of the CPSU and Ourselves," *NCNA*, September 6, 1963.

[7] First charged in the Chinese government statement of August 15, 1963, (*NCNA* same date) and repeated in the joint editorial of September 6 cited in the preceding note.

[8] For an account of the Sino-Soviet exchanges preceding the *TASS* statement of September 9, 1959, see the *People's Daily* editorial of November 2, 1963, "The Truth about How the Leaders of the CPSU Have Allied Themselves with India against China."

he and Mao Tse-tung disagreed on the value of his American visit, on China's demands against India, and on Khrushchev's suggestion that it would be worth China's while to
get the Americans out of Taiwan as Lenin had got the Japanese out of Siberia—by setting up a buffer state, the
"Far Eastern Republic," with their consent; [9] they also
disagreed on Khrushchev's advice to the Algerian Nationalists to take up de Gaulle's offer of self-determina-
tion as a basis for negotiation.[10]

The difference of emphasis had given rise to different
policies over a wide range of issues. The disappointment
of the Chinese leaders at their inability to influence their
powerful ally on these issues now combined with other
causes of dissatisfaction, as well as with an older conviction of their own superiority in the ideological field, to
cause them to launch an ideological debate, throughout the
Communist world movement, in which these differences
were presented in generalized form—as a dispute between
orthodox Leninism and "modern revisionism." Following
a preparatory phase during the winter of 1959–60, the Chinese platform for the attack was published on the 90th
anniversary of Lenin's birth, in April, 1960.[11] From this
time dates the public dispute on "the inevitability of war,"
the role of peaceful coexistence as a "general line" or a
tactic subordinated to the struggle against imperialism,
the need to mobilize the masses for peace rather than to
"beg the imperialists for peace," and the danger of spread-
ing illusions about the chances of general and complete
disarmament instead of preparing the oppressed nations
for armed struggle.

[9] Chinese government statement of September 1, 1963, *NCNA* same
date.

[10] Cf. the opposite statements on de Gaulle's proposals in *NCNA*,
October 17, 1959, and in Khrushchev's address to the Supreme Soviet,
Moscow Radio, October 31, 1959.

[11] See in particular the *Red Flag* article "Long Live Leninism,"
translated in *Peking Review*, No. 17, 1960.

Yet if Leninist verbiage and deliberate distortion are stripped away, there remain the same issues of substance: a Chinese willingness to push local revolutionary conflicts, regardless of risks, versus a Soviet determination to keep the risk of escalation under control at any moment; and a Soviet readiness to use the machineries of summit diplomacy, of the United Nations and of negotiations in general, as important levers for their general pressure toward their objectives—along with military threats and revolutionary movements—and also as instruments for limiting the risks of the latter, versus a Chinese conviction that diplomacy could only be used either as a form of propaganda or for formalizing results already achieved by revolutionary force.

II

From what has been said so far, it follows that the Chinese launched the "ideological dispute" because, during the years 1958–59, they had failed to exercise effective pressure on Soviet foreign policy by other means. There are indications that in the period between the opening of the public debate in April, 1960, and the temporary compromise achieved at the Moscow world conference of Communist parties at the end of that year, their pressure did make some impact in the desired direction.[12]

Their attack in April—seconded, as we know now, by Molotov, who sent an article on similar lines to the Moscow "Kommunist" from his Mongolian post [13]—came on the eve of a Four-Power "summit conference" planned for May. It coincided with several speeches by senior American officials which indicated clearly that the hope of major U.S.

---

[12] Cf. my paper quoted in note 3 above.
[13] Disclosed by Ilyichev in his speech at the Twenty-second Congress of the CPSU, October 24, 1961.

concessions on the Berlin issue, which Khrushchev had carried home from Camp David, had no chance of being fulfilled. Unless the Soviet Premier could force the American President to disavow his advisers at the last moment, this left him with the prospect of a summit deadlock on the issue on which he had staked his prestige, and of discussion concentrating only on the issues of disarmament and an atomic test ban on which he was under acute Chinese attack.

It was at this moment that the U–2 incident provided him with a way out. Whether his violent reaction was a serious attempt to differentiate between Eisenhower and his advisers or whether it was meant from the start to prepare a refusal to attend the conference, the President's assumption of personal responsibility certainly facilitated the latter decision. While Chinese pressure would hardly have been strong enough to prevent Khrushchev from picking a Berlin victory from the conference table, it did probably contribute to making him abandon a conference where no such victory was on offer.

During the following months, and particularly after Khrushchev's counterattack on the Chinese during the Rumanian party congress at Bucharest had failed to bring a decision, and preparations for the Moscow world conference had begun, Soviet policy toward the West became markedly more negative and rhetorical. It took no greater risks than previously—the Berlin question was adjourned pending the election of a new American president. But there was no more serious effort at negotiation in any field: the talks on an atomic test ban dragged on in utter futility, while the Soviets left the ten-power disarmament negotiations—immediately after Bucharest—just when the Western powers were about to present the proposals for which the Soviets had called. Above all, the Soviets reacted to the outbreak of the Congo troubles with denunciations of an alleged joint neo-colonialist plot of the Western powers that were remarkable for their rhetorical violence and absurdity, even by Communist standards; and Khrushchev himself used the first open conflict between Castro and the United States to threaten the latter with rockets— though in both cases he took good care to avoid any actual risk. In the Congo, in Cuba, and in Khrushchev's personal performance at the United Nations in that autumn, the Soviets were at such pains to prove themselves as powerful and intrepid champions of anti-colonialism that the impression can scarcely be avoided that they were trying largely, in preparation for the Moscow conference, to convince their own followers that the Chinese charges were unfounded.

Yet even during these months of intense ideological competition within the Communist world movement, Soviet policy toward the West was influenced more in its gestures than in its substance, and more in the passive failure to negotiate than in the active assumption of risks. And after the December compromise of 1960, in which the Soviets had not only secured the backing of the huge majority of Communist parties but had used the opportunity of formally laying down the "leading role" in the world movement,[14] with its attendant awkward responsibility, these limited effects of Chinese pressure were also fast to disappear. In 1961, while struggling vainly behind the scenes to liquidate the Chinese outpost in Albania, the Soviets' Western policy appeared to be guided wholly by their own interests—above all by their effort to force a break-through in Berlin; the resumption of tests in the multimegaton range on the eve of their Twenty-second Party Congress seems also to call for interpretation in the German rather than in the Chinese context.

Nor did the breakdown of the 1960 compromise at that congress make any visible difference to Soviet policy to-

---

[14] See Khrushchev's report on the 1960 Moscow conference quoted in note 2 above.

ward the West: the Soviets went ahead pursuing their own aims, and nothing in their subsequent behavior toward the West seems to require an explanation in Chinese terms. Certainly the Cuban adventure of the fall of 1962 cannot be viewed as a repetition of the violent gestures of 1960: it was much more serious but much less rhetorical—undertaken not to demonstrate solidarity with Cuba, but to use Cuba for a surprise improvement of Russia's strategic position. Impatient at the failure of their attempts to disintegrate the Western Alliance by nuclear blackmail, the Soviets had decided to try and increase the strength of the blackmail at considerable risk. They had done so without consulting China,[15] and when the risk proved too high, they withdrew in the teeth of Chinese cries of "appeasement."

III

It may be assumed that the Cuban defeat proved a turning point in Soviet strategy.[16] The estimate that the balance of nuclear power would permit a disintegration of the Western Alliance and, hence, a decisive advance of Communist political power without serious risk of world war— formulated in the Moscow declaration of 1960 and the CPSU program of 1961 as the arrival of a "third stage of the general crisis of capitalism" without world war—had to be revised. The offensive based on this estimate, notably the attempt to force a solution at Berlin, had to be abandoned. The armament race caused by this offensive had to be stopped as too costly. A new attempt had to be made to inaugurate a phase of reduced international tension, and to concentrate on increasing the internal stability of the

---

[15] This has been stated, e.g., in the Chinese government statement of September 1, 1963, *NCNA*, same date.

[16] For a fuller statement of the argument of this paragraph see R. Lowenthal, "The End of an Illusion?," *Problems of Communism*, Vol. XII, No. 1 (January-February, 1963).

Soviet empire by economic improvements for the masses, notably by increased investments in agriculture. In November, 1962, the CPSU was told that its primary task was in the economic field, and was reorganized accordingly.[17]

This turn was bound to widen the gulf between Soviet and Chinese policies toward the West. The Chinese had criticized the Soviets for not taking sufficiently bold risks in their offensive; they were bound to talk of betrayal once the offensive was called off without success. It seems likely that this consideration delayed the open proclamation of the turn: the Soviet party and the Communist world movement had to be prepared. The turn was proclaimed when the Soviets decided to sign the partial ban on atomic tests, on terms virtually identical with those proposed by the Western powers, in August, 1962. It was done in July, 1963—nine months after Cuba, and only after the "bilateral talks" with the Chinese party delegation had failed and the documents been published. But the talks had not been a serious attempt to reach a new compromise: both sides had only maneuvered to fix the responsibility for a split that both regarded as inevitable.

Since then, the full development of both platforms for the split and the efforts of both sides to prepare for a new world conference—or more probably two rival world conferences—have coincided with a virtual standstill in Soviet policy toward the West. As in the months preceding the 1960 world conference, Soviet foreign policy has to take into account not the interests of China, but the need to compete with her for the allegiance of Communists all over the world; and while this competition does not now produce such rhetorical excesses on the Soviet side as it did then, it hampers the Soviets' freedom of movement. In the short run, the effect of the open split has been, and may still be for some time, to delay the full unfolding of the

---

[17] See Khrushchev's report to the November, 1962, plenum of the Central Committee of the CPSU, *Moscow Radio*, November 21, 1962.

new line in Soviet foreign policy—to make Soviet diplomacy go somewhat slower on proposals for arms limitation, etc., than it would otherwise do.

Yet as the decision to make the turn has nevertheless been taken and is to be carried through under Chinese ideological fire, it has to be justified in ideological terms; and this may tend in the medium-long run to make the turn rather more far-reaching—rather less tactical and more profound—that it would otherwise be. In trying to systematize their diverging policies, Chinese and Soviet Communists have come to stress opposite aspects of the Leninist synthesis to a point that seems to be leading straight to its disintegration. Lenin had transformed the Marxist belief in the necessary development of modern industrial society toward proletarian socialism and communism into a strategy proclaiming the immediate urgency of the Communist seizure of power and the revolutionary alliance between the proletariat of the industrial West and the nationalist movements of the colonial and semicolonial countries; but he had never abandoned his conviction that the industrial proletariat was the basic force of the world revolution. Yet after decades in which the Communists have failed to seize power in any advanced industrial country (except under the impact of Soviet military expansion) but have achieved revolutionary victories in various parts of the underdeveloped world, it has become extremely difficult to maintain Lenin's beliefs in the urgency of revolution and in the leading role of the industrial proletariat at the same time.

The Chinese, clearly giving preference to the urgency of revolution and civil war, have logically arrived at the thesis that the underdeveloped regions of Asia, Africa, and Latin America are today "the main focus of world contradictions," and that their revolutions may be "decisive" even for the victory of the proletariat in the advanced countries.[18] Conversely, the Soviets have not only charged them with a "racialist" tendency to isolate the anticolonial movements from the main force of the "socialist camp" and the industrial proletariat,[19] but have increasingly stressed the Marxist arguments concerning the economic preconditions of socialist and Communist construction, to a point where in the latest Soviet theoretical pronouncements the economic advance in the building of communism appears as the principal international duty of the CPSU.[20]

It makes, of course, a big difference whether this "competitive" aspect of coexistence is stressed in speeches and interviews for the benefit of the Western public—which has long been the case—or whether the Soviet cadres themselves are told on theoretical grounds that they will fulfill their international responsibilities best by building up a happy and prosperous model society at home. Khrushchev and Suslov, who had felt strong enough to transcend Stalin's "socialism in one country" by using their world position to promote a rapid advance of world revolution, are thus driven back, partly by the successes of Western resistance and partly by the logic of their dispute with China, to envisage the building of "communism in one empire."

This new tendency of the Soviet Communist leaders to proclaim domestic economic progress as the principal task of their party goes beyond the tactical sphere and could, if continued, eventually lead to more lasting changes in the

---

[18] This view was first spelled out in the *Red Flag* editorial of March 4, 1963, "More on the Differences between Comrade Togliatti and Us," and repeated in the "Proposal for the General Line of the Communist Movement" addressed to the Central Committee of the CPSU by the Central Committee on the CPC on June 14, 1963; see also the fourth joint editorial of *Red Flag* and *People's Daily*, "Apologists of Neo-Colonialism," *NCNA*, October 22, 1963.

[19] First in the "Open Letter" published by the Central Committee of the CPSU, on July 14, 1963.

[20] Thus M. N. Suslov's report to the Central Committee of the CPSU, rendered on February 14, 1964, and published in *Pravda*, April 3, 1964.

character of Soviet foreign policy. But it is fraught with immense difficulties, because it seems to involve nothing less than an attempt to change the legitimation of the party dictatorship—and to change it in a direction that is rather against its nature. It is natural for a totalitarian regime to justify itself by the need for ever new forced transformations of society at home and for permanent conflict abroad; it is far less plausible to argue that the rule of an ideological party is the best means for promoting the growth of a peaceful welfare state. We must therefore expect that the party machine will, from instinct of self-preservation no less than from ideological tradition, resist the tendency to change its legitimation so thoroughly, and will tend to cling to the sense of security it derives at home from an atmosphere of permanent conflict abroad.

On the other hand, the pressure toward a devaluation of the ideological as compared with the material tasks is inherent in the present stage of development of Soviet society, and the more the party tries to resist this pressure and to cling to its traditional ideological legitimation, the more it risks to be isolated from the living forces of society and to find its position weakened in the next succession crisis. The conflict with China, following on the blows that the de-Stalinization and the Hungarian revolution inflicted on the Party's authority, must have further weakened the former unquestioning faith in communism as a world-wide doctrine among the intellectual and administrative elites of the Soviet Union, and must have raised widespread doubts about the continued relevance of that doctrine for the greatness of Russia. Whether the party adjusts itself to this current by increasingly stressing its pragmatic economic tasks or whether it resists it and is eventually relegated to a less powerful role—as Malenkov seems to have intended after Stalin's death—the long-run effect of the Sino-Soviet schism is likely to weaken the Soviet regime's drive for world-wide expansion and its sense of permanent conflict with the non-Communist world, and to push it into the direction of more nearly "normal," i.e., more limited and national, power politics.

IV

More immediately, the Communist schism has changed the policies and prospects of every Communist party in the world, and will continue to do so in the future.

In Eastern Europe, the dispute has increased the scope for the pursuit of independent policies by the ruling Communist parties in the short run. It is, for instance, highly unlikely that the Rumanian Communists would have dared to oppose Soviet proposals for integrated East European planning in the way they did unless they felt that the Soviets would hesitate to take drastic measures against them while they were competing with Peking for support in the Communist world movement.

To some extent, this is a passing situation: once the split between Moscow and Peking is formally accomplished, the Soviets may try to tighten the reins again. The East European Communists are fully aware of that, and this is one main reason why many of them have sought to postpone the evil day and have preached conciliation in the teeth of all evidence of an unbridgeable gulf.

Yet it is doubtful whether the greater relative independence gained by the one-time satellite regimes in recent years can be easily destroyed by the Soviets, even after a formal break with China. After all, by showing more independence these regimes have broadened their basis of domestic support; and by increasing their domestic support, they have gained a better foundation for standing up for their specific national interests against the Kremlin. The permanent weakening of Soviet authority by the mere fact of the split—the permanent destruction of the myth of the uniqueness of the Soviet Union—will further help the East European Communists in resisting Soviet demands. Whether or not demonstrations of independence of the Rumanian type will be repeated, there will certainly be no return to Stalinist discipline within the bloc.

Outside it, Yugoslavia, while cordially welcoming the break with Peking, shows little inclination to return to a Moscow-centered international Communist organization. More important, the Western Communist parties, while generally on Russia's side in the dispute with China, seem the less eager for a new Moscow-run International the more confidence they have in their own ability to conduct a successful policy. It is the former loyal Stalinist parties, who regard blind obedience to Moscow as a basic article of their faith, who are today loyal followers of Khrushchev's "anti-Stalinist" line and willing to join any new organization Moscow may devise; this goes above all for the French Communists, and equally for some of the weakest and most isolated Western Communist parties. Conversely, it is the ably-led parties that most genuinely welcomed the beginnings of de-Stalinization, above all the Italian party, that are now reticent about the idea of a new Moscow-run world conference.

In fact, the prospects of communism in the advanced Western countries have probably been damaged beyond repair. If the parties in these countries cling to Soviet authority as if nothing had happened, they will increasingly isolate themselves from national life. If they try to strike out on a road of their own in an atmosphere of democratic discussion, they may find that adjustments they make for tactical reasons are taken seriously by their own members until they are transformed, against the intentions of their leaders, into radical parties of a democratic left-wing opposition—a fate of which some indications are already noticeable in the Italian case. The choice is between hopeless ossification and a revisionism that may easily get out of hand.

V

Any realistic discussion on how the West could consciously influence or exploit the Sino-Soviet dispute must start with the question of how far the West has influenced its course already—without necessarily meaning to do so. At least three examples come to mind.

First, during the Quemoy crisis of 1958, American technological support to the Chinese nationalists, given in a defensive framework, combined with the danger of possible direct American intervention to raise the risk of escalation to a point where the Soviets preferred to limit their own support for Peking. A lesser American involvement might have encouraged continued Soviet backing for the Chinese Communist offensive; a more direct American participation might have forced the Soviets to defend Communist China against a supposed American threat. The actual dosage, chosen because it was just sufficient to repel the Chinese attack, had the incidental effect of making Peking feel that Moscow was doing less for its allies than Washington, and of making Moscow conscious of the need to control Chinese forwardness and if possible bring about a negotiated solution for Taiwan. It thus contributed to the growth of the dispute.

Second, Anglo-American willingness to negotiate a nuclear test ban, with its implication of interest also in a non-proliferation agreement, has made it easier for the Soviets to refuse the handing over of atomic bombs or production designs to Peking; by the same token, it has made Chinese distrust of any negotiations between the Soviets and the Western powers far more acute from the moment in 1959 when this refusal was first pronounced. The successive decisions of the Western governments to reduce their inspection requirements to the minimum compatible with their security, and finally to offer an uninspected partial ban excluding underground tests, increased the inducement for the Soviets to sign the agreement though they knew it would be regarded by Peking as directed against its interests. Its actual signature amounted to a Soviet declaration of independence from Chinese pressure and was answered by Chinese charges of betrayal and Chinese disclosure of past internal negotiations. Thus Western diplomacy in this field substantially contributed to sharpening the dispute and to increasing Soviet awareness of the common interests of Russia and the West in reducing the risks of nuclear war.

Third, Western firmness in resisting Soviet demands for a change in the status of West Berlin and for signing peace treaties with "the two German states," followed by American firmness in dealing with Khrushchev's missile installation in Cuba, have finally convinced the Soviet leaders that the risk involved in their policy of nuclear blackmail was too serious to push it any further. Soviet determination not to yield to the Chinese arguments in favor of still bolder risk-taking has been correspondingly strengthened, and so has the Chinese belief that the Soviet leaders lack the courage to use the opportunities offered by the present world situation. Again, the Soviet retreat from Cuba and the effective dropping of the Berlin crisis contributed to exacerbate the dispute and forced the Soviet leaders publicly to commit themselves to a policy of increased caution and "reasonableness."

It will be observed that the above three examples of successful Western policies fit neither a general prescription for "toughness" nor for "softness"—neither the idea that the West must "help" Khrushchev against the Chinese (and against a supposed "Stalinist" opposition within the present Soviet leadership) nor the idea that it must never make any concession. Both Western firmness on Berlin and Cuba and partial Western concessions on the terms for the test ban, as well as the fact of American aid for the Chinese Nationalists and the limitations of that aid, seem to have contributed to foiling the Communist offensive and to driving its two centers farther and farther apart. This is, of course, not surprising, since general "toughness" or "softness" are emotional slogans rather than prescriptions for a rational political strategy; the actual decisions on Western policy had to be reached from a study of the interests involved in each particular issue rather than from a choice between "ideological" generalities.

Yet—and here is the crucial point—the interests in the light of which Western policy had to be determined in each particular case were primarily the Western powers' own interests. Just what the United States could do in the Quemoy crisis depended primarily on its estimate of the balance of risks involved in alternative courses. How far the U.S. and Britain could go in reducing the inspection requirements for a nuclear test ban depended on the best technical advice about what their security required. The impossibility of yielding on Berlin resulted from its importance for the cohesion of the Western Alliance; the need for quick and decisive action against the missile installation in Cuba followed from the clear and present danger to American and hemispheric security. In every case, considerations of the likely effects on Sino-Russian relations, if present at all, must have been secondary to the decisive impact of direct Western interests.

Obviously, the same is bound to be true in the future. The West may make some small specific moves with the Sino-Soviet dispute primarily in mind, such as extending diplomatic recognition to the Mongolian Peoples' Republic or improving trade relations with Albania. But on the big issues, such as diplomatic relations with Peking or the main subjects under negotiation with the U.S.S.R., major Western interests are bound to outweigh any complicated tactical calculations of possible indirect effects on the dispute.

The real question, then, is how the West can take advantage of the changes in Soviet policy and in the East European situation likely to flow from the dispute. To a large extent, this question forms the subject of the papers dealing with the effects of the relaxation of tension and with the problems of Central Europe. But some general remarks may be in order in the present context.

In the first place, it is clearly in the Western interest to help the East European Communist states in preserving the greater independence they have gained in recent years, and particularly in resisting Soviet pressure toward a more strictly integrated division of labor within the bloc. This means that the West is interested in using the present détente not only to extend contacts with Eastern Europe in general, but specifically to extend trade with the countries in process of de-satellization and even to grant them credits, and that the trade policy of the West European Common Market should take this into account. It also means that it is greatly in the interest of the West that the German Federal Republic—the major Western country nearest to these states and traditionally linked with their economies—should make every effort to turn itself from a bogeyman for these countries into a bridge toward them. The creation of West German trade missions in most of these countries has been a useful step in the right direction, but major progress will be impossible without a visible change in the Federal Republic's attitude to Germany's eastern frontier. This does not require that Bonn should abandon its legal reservation on this matter: the view that the frontier can only be formally recognized in an all-German peace treaty is perfectly justified as far as it goes. But it does require that Bonn's general political pronouncements and propaganist activities should give the impression that it is realistically resigned to the fact that such a treaty could only confirm the present Oder-Neisse frontier in its essentials—instead of persistently giving the opposite impression of an illusory belief that substantial changes could one day be achieved, and thus objectively helping the Soviets in keeping alive the fear of German "revanchism."

In the second place, Western policy toward the Soviet Union should be conducted both with short-run power relations and with the promotion of long-run changes in mind. Of course the West can at best exert a limited influence on these long-run internal developments, and it cannot afford to make unilateral concessions in the present in the hope of possible compensatory gains in the future. But in a situation of relative détente, i.e., in the absence of acute East-West crises, the West can and should foster every form of contact with the Soviet Union —economic, cultural, and touristic—that involves no such unilateral concessions. For the more Soviet people are involved in such contacts with the West, the more the hold of the official monopoly of information will be weakened and the more difficult will the Party's efforts to preserve ideological uniformity be made. This is certainly no reason to abandon the control of trade in strategic goods, nor to ease the Soviets' problem of investment priorities by granting them long-term credits; in this latter respect, our attitude to the Soviets should be different from that to the smaller East European nations. But in general it is true that the lowering of barriers during a period of détente is in the long-run interest of the West.

The Sino-Soviet Dispute and the West: The Chinese Aspect

by
Harold C. Hinton*

In recent years Communist China's behavior has been
so unconventional as to evoke in many quarters the familiar charge of irrationality, the last resort of the uncompre-
hending. In essence, the problem arises out of the
complex and shifting blend of modern totalitarianism and
the contemporary incarnation of the world's most integrated and durable traditional civilization. The confusion
has been compounded by the astounding but undeniable
fact that, despite its obvious internal weaknesses, China
has made substantial gains in its bizarre contest with its
various opponents. The confusion is not inescapable, however, for to those who can and will read there are available a number of excellent studies that go far toward
clarifying the nature of the Chinese Communists' aims

* *Harold C. Hinton:* Senior staff member, Institute for Defense
Analyses, Washington, D. C.; Associate Professor of Political Science,
The George Washington University; co-author, *Major Governments of
Asia* (Cornell University Press, 1958 and 1963); author, *Communist
China in World Politics* (Houghton Mifflin, forthcoming).

and methods, at any rate with regard to the Sino-Soviet dispute.[1]

The Impact of Détente on the Sino-Soviet Alliance

Like the Communist portions of the other divided countries—Germany, Korea, and Vietnam—Communist China has strong militant tendencies, and for understandable reasons. More than the others, it sees itself as overwhelmingly superior to its non-Communist rival. At least as much as the others, it finds itself prevented from asserting that superiority by the military power of the United States. Worse still, the United States and Nationalist China pose, or seem to pose, a serious threat to the very existence of the Communist Chinese regime. Many of the latter's goals —in particular its desire to create buffer states along its border and ultimately to exercise some form of hegemony over the whole of Asia—also find American opposition to be their major single obstacle.

In this situation, and for other reasons as well, Communist China turned in the first months of its existence to the Soviet Union. From the Russians it sought, among other things, economic and military aid, protection against attack, diversionary pressures on the United States (ideally in Europe), and political and diplomatic support. To a significant but far from unlimited degree, the Chinese received these things from Stalin. In a sense, the Cold War was Peking's shield.

Even Stalin in his last years tended to relax his pressures on the West somewhat, in an effort to split it.[2] His

---

[1] The writer has in mind in particular the writings of Zbigniew Brzezinski, William E. Griffith, Richard Lowenthal, Benjamin Schwartz, Allen S. Whiting, and Donald S. Zagoria. See also the excellent anonymous study, "The Sino-Soviet Dispute in Chinese Perspective," *Current Scene* (Hong Kong), Vol. II, No. 17 (July 15, 1963).

[2] Cf. Marshall D. Shulman, *Stalin's Foreign Policy Reappraised* (Cambridge, Mass.: Harvard University Press, 1963).

successors, influenced among other things by the diminishing blackmail value of the Soviet military threat to Western Europe in the face of the emergence of American thermonuclear and tactical nuclear weapons in 1954, went much further. It seems fair to say that Beria, Malenkov, and Khrushchev successively promoted a kind of détente with the West as the only safe course. This policy of détente has been subject to two main qualifications of importance. One is that the Soviet Union must occasionally do something to keep alive, in both Communist and non-Communist eyes, its reputation as a promoter of world revolution. The other is that the Soviet Union is determined to prevent the reunification of Germany except on its own terms and under Communist control. Of these two considerations, the second is the only one over which the Soviet Union has shown a willingness to expose itself to serious military risk.[3] At no time has the Soviet Union incurred such a risk primarily for the sake of its Chinese ally.[4] The Soviet Union, to be sure, would probably feel compelled to respond with more than words or token actions if the United States should land troops in Chinese territory near the Soviet border or launch an unprovoked strategic air attack against Communist China. Such contingencies are extremely remote, however, and in any sort of realistically likely encounter between Communist China and the United States the Soviet Union, with a keen

[3] Soviet missiles were sent into Cuba in all probability in order to coerce the United States, after the congressional elections, into agreeing to a German settlement on Khrushchev's terms. For evidence, see the Soviet statement of September 11, 1962 (in *The New York Times,* September 12, 1962). See also Arnold L. Horelick, "The Cuban Missile Crisis: An Analysis of Soviet Calculations and Behavior," *World Politics,* Vol. XVI, No. 3 (April, 1964), pp. 363–89.

[4] On Soviet unwillingness to incur any genuine risk at the time of the Quemoy crisis of 1958, see John R. Thomas, "Soviet Behavior in the Quemoy Crisis of 1958," *Orbis,* Vol. VI, No. 1 (Spring, 1962), pp. 38–64.

eye to its own survival, would probably confine its reaction to a minimal level.[5]

The delicate plant of the Sino-Soviet alliance has tended to wilt in the warm, if intermittent and unreliable, sunshine of Soviet-Western détente. The Chinese have felt increasingly uncertain, or even deprived, of the aid, protection, diversionary pressures, and political support that were their main objectives when they allied themselves with the Soviet Union.

Major developments in the Soviet-Western détente, and in particular Soviet disarmament maneuvers with adverse implications for Chinese security, have often been accompanied by convulsions in Communist China's domestic and/or foreign policy. The Geneva summit conference of July, 1955, probably contributed to the sudden decision greatly to accelerate the socialization and industrialization of the Chinese economy. The Soviet Twentieth Congress of February, 1956, whose proceedings were permeated with a fear of nuclear war masquerading under the rubric of "noninevitability," certainly contributed to the decision, taken in the same year, that Communist China must acquire nuclear weapons of its own.[6] Khrushchev exploited his triumphs in military and space technology in 1957, not, as the Chinese urged, to blackmail the West, but to cajole it (with indifferent success) into negotiations. At the end

---

[5] The Soviet press implied as much in 1962, on the occasion of the twenty-fifth anniversary of the outbreak of the Sino-Japanese War.

[6] Cf. Defense Minister P'eng Te-huai's formulation of the desired military posture, in his report to the Chinese Eighth Party Congress: "People's armed forces handling modern weapons" (New China News Agency dispatch, September 19, 1956). Note the following remark by Khrushchev to the Twentieth Congress: "Prior to agreement on the major aspects of disarmament, we are willing to take certain partial steps in this sphere—for example, to discontinue thermonuclear weapon tests. . . ." (in Current Soviet Policies—II [New York: Praeger, 1957], p. 35. Khrushchev also began his "rocket rattling" in 1956, but these were essentially empty threats for political effect and so timed as to not create serious military risk.

of March, 1958, Khrushchev inaugurated a unilateral suspension of nuclear testing, with the announced purpose of
minimizing the chances of nuclear diffusion. Although
his main intended target was almost certainly West Germany, the implications were adverse to Communist China
as well.[7] This development, coming at a time when the
armed forces of Nationalist China were being rapidly
strengthened through American aid, was probably a major
contributor to at least some features of the "Great Leap
Forward," and in particular the "backyard steel" campaign and the militia campaign.[8] At about this time the
Communist Chinese adopted the disarmament policy to
which they still cling: complete, uninspected *nuclear* disarmament, without conventional disarmament.[9] The im-
plementation of this demand would, of course, leave China
the strongest military power in Asia.

By the beginning of 1959, Khrushchev had made clear
the low priority he attached to the Sino-Soviet alliance, as
compared with his goals of achieving a Berlin settlement,
preventing West Germany's acquisition of nuclear weapons, and then proceeding with a détente with the West
as a cover for his policy of allegedly "peaceful competi-

---

[7] It should be noted that the Soviet Union had committed itself in
October, 1957, to a modest program of aid to China in the production
of nuclear weapons (Chinese statement released by New China News
Agency, August 15, 1963).

[8] On the Chinese Nationalist military buildup, see Joyce Kallgren,
"Nationalist China's Armed Forces," *The China Quarterly*, No. 15
(July–September, 1963), p. 38. Tito's support, whether in spite of or
because of his "revisionist" tendencies, for Khrushchev's foreign policy
at this time was probably one of the main reasons why the Chinese
launched a propaganda offensive against Tito, beginning with "Modern
Revisionism Must Be Repudiated," *People's Daily*, May 5, 1958. On
the "backyard steel" campaign, see Richard Moorsteen, *An Economic
Development of Strategic Importance in Communist China* (The
RAND Corporation, Paper P–1578, December 15, 1958). On the militia
campaign, see Ralph L. Powell, "Everyone a Soldier: The Communist
Chinese Militia," *Foreign Affairs*, October, 1960, pp. 100–11.

[9] Cf. Alice Langley Hsieh, *Communist China's Strategy in the Nuclear Era* (Englewood Cliffs, N.J.: Prentice-Hall, 1962), pp. 104–5.

tion with capitalism." To the Chinese, on the other hand, the Sino-Soviet alliance remained at the top of the agenda, even if their own behavior was not of the kind most likely to insure Soviet good will and protection. In the military field, Khrushchev was offering the Chinese little but a series of vague proposals for an atom-free zone in the Far East and the Pacific. In May, 1959, when Khrushchev failed to enforce his "ultimatum" on Berlin even after the resignation and death of the formidable John Foster Dulles, it became clear that the Chinese could no longer hope for direct Soviet pressures on the United States in Europe that would effectively distract it from the Far East. In June, Khrushchev terminated his modest program of aid to the Chinese in the development of nuclear weapons, allegedly in order to improve the prospects for better relations with the United States.[10]

Other events, literally too numerous to mention, rocked the Sino-Soviet alliance to its foundations during 1959, and yet the Chinese continued to publish only indirect criticisms of Soviet policy. Under the consciously misleading guise of a debate over the *effects* of thermonuclear war, they had been lecturing the Russians on its *likelihood,* which they regarded (and regard) as lower than do the Russians. This being the case, the Chinese wanted the Communist bloc, and especially the Soviet Union in view of its power, actively to support "national revolutionary movements" in the underdeveloped areas.[11] The tenth an-

---

[10] Chinese statement of August 15, 1963 (see note 7).

[11] The revolutionary strategy preferred by the Chinese, and projected to a large extent on the basis of their interpretation of their own rise to power, runs in brief as follows: A given Communist party forms a fairly broad "anti-imperialist united front" under its own leadership, combats its foreign and domestic enemies by vigorous means that typically include "armed struggle," provokes if necessary some form of "imperialist" intervention so as to educate its people by the powerful force of negative example, and uses the ensuing crisis as a cover under which successively to subdue or eliminate the non-Communist elements of the united front and gain undivided power (for a good

niversary of the Sino-Soviet alliance (February 14, 1960) was celebrated with correctness on both sides and with effusiveness on the Chinese, although Khrushchev spent the day in New Delhi.[12] This was a deceptive calm, however. Despite an official, explicit Chinese warning on January 21 against any such procedure, the Soviet Union attempted, at the Ten-Nation Disarmament Conference in Geneva in the spring, to bind Communist China, in its absence, to a disarmament agreement by proposing that the conventional forces of the United States and the two major Communist powers be pegged at 1.7 million men each. The Chinese retaliated by launching their first major, public propaganda attack against Soviet ideology and strategy on April 16.[13]

This in turn set in motion a rapid escalation of the Sino-Soviet dispute, into the details of which there is no space to enter.[14] Meanwhile Khrushchev continued to follow his chosen path, notoriously erratic though it was, of "peaceful competition with capitalism," modified by the two considerations mentioned earlier. The Chinese still entertained hopes of revivifying the alliance, however, and the

---

summary see "The Sino-Soviet Dispute in Chinese Perspective," *op. cit.*). The Chinese are flexible enough, however, to accept the fact that in many countries the only attainable approximation to this process will be a revolution under the leadership of a non-Communist, although leftist, "national democratic" movement. Such a situation the Chinese regard as acceptable, pending the presumably hoped-for time when the regime becomes fully Communist, to the extent that it is anti-Soviet as well as anti-American (for evidence, see "Apologists of Neocolonialism," *People's Daily* and *Red Flag*, October 22, 1963).

[12] American Consulate General, Hong Kong, "Tenth Anniversary of Signing of Sino-Soviet Treaty of Friendship, Alliance, and Mutual Assistance," *Current Background*, No. 613 (February 26, 1960).

[13] "Long Live Leninism!" *Red Flag*, April 16, 1960. April 22 was the ninetieth anniversary of Lenin's birth.

[14] See Harry Gelman, "The Conflict: A Survey," *Problems of Communism*, Vol. XIII, No. 2 (March–April, 1964), pp. 3–15.

Russians were not above playing on this hope as a means of restraining Chinese political pressures on themselves.[15]

In the spring of 1962, more or less simultaneously, the Chinese Nationalists made what looked like preparations for an invasion of the mainland, and the Soviet Union began to lend support to dissident Kazakhs in the Chinese province of Sinkiang, near the border of Soviet Central Asia.[16] With purely nominal Soviet support, the Communist Chinese effectively deterred a Nationalist invasion, if one was in fact contemplated, and even secured from the United States a pledge not to aid such an invasion if it should occur.[17] This in turn made it possible for the Chinese to turn to the Himalayas and to begin (in July) building up military pressures on the Indian Army. The purpose was mainly to deter further Indian advances in the disputed regions along the frontier, and secondarily to retaliate for certain political acts of the Indian government, such as its increasingly anti-Communist role as chairman of the International Control Commission on Vietnam.

The Chinese probably hoped that the tense Berlin and German situations, and above all the flow of Soviet arms

---

[15] In an unprecedented formula, Marshal Malinovsky declared in January, 1962, that the Soviet Union would defend "socialist countries friendly to us" (quoted in Thomas, "Soviet Behavior in the Quemoy Crisis of 1958," p. 64). This statement was followed by a brief improvement in Sino-Soviet state, although not party, relations.

[16] "In April and May, 1962, the leaders of the CPSU used their organs and personnel in Sinkiang, China, to carry out large-scale subversive activities in the Ili region and enticed and coerced several tens of thousands of Chinese citizens into going to the Soviet Union. The Chinese government lodged repeated protests and made repeated representations, but the Soviet government refused to repatriate these Chinese citizens on the pretext 'of the sense of Soviet legality' and 'humanitarianism.' To this day this incident remains unsettled. This is indeed an astounding event, unheard of in relations between socialist countries" ("The Origin and Development of the Differences Between the Leadership of the CPSU and Ourselves," *People's Daily* and *Red Flag*, September 6, 1963).

[17] See *The New York Times*, June 27, 1962.

into Cuba after July, would divert the attention of both the United States and the Soviet Union from the Himalayas and might even put an end once for all to the over-all trend toward a Soviet-American détente. This in turn might lead the Soviet Union to observe what the Chinese regarded as its obligations under the Sino-Soviet alliance. It is reasonable to suppose that the Chinese expected such a trend to be associated with the fall of Khrushchev and his replacement by a successor somewhat closer to the Chinese point of view, presumably Kozlov.[18] When the Sino-Indian border and the Cuban situations assumed crisis proportions, on October 20 and 22 respectively, Communist China and the Soviet preserved, of necessity, a reasonable parallelism in their public pronouncements for a few days.[19] This ended as soon as it became clear, on October 26, that Khrushchev was going to capitulate over Cuba, The following day the *People's Daily* demanded in strong language that the Soviet Union, as well as the Indian Commu-

---

[18] Note the following Chinese warning to the Soviet leadership against Khrushchev's "modern revisionism," at a time when his chosen successor Brezhnev had just paid a visit to the man whom the Chinese regard as the founder of "modern revisionism," Tito: "The imperialists, the reactionaries of various countries, and the modern revisionists have engaged in all kinds of criminal activities to oppose communism, oppose the people, oppose the mass struggle of all oppressed nations and oppose the People's Republic of China and all other independent countries in Asia, Africa, Latin America and elsewhere, which refuse to be slaves, but the result is contrary to their expectations . . . the revolutionary cause of the people of all countries continues to develop, the international Communist movement is growing daily in strength, and our friends have become more numerous" (communiqué of the Tenth Plenary Session of the Chinese Party's Central Committee, New China News Agency dispatch, September 28, 1962). The writer regards Khrushchev's domestic political difficulties at that time as established in the important but controversial article by Carl Linden, "Khrushchev and the Party Battle," *Problems of Communism,* Vol. XII, No. 5 (September–October, 1963), pp. 27–35.

[19] On the Sino-Indian conflict, compare the Chinese and Soviet statements of October 24 and October 25, respectively. On the Cuban crisis, compare the Soviet and Chinese statements of October 23 and October 25, respectively.

nists, repudiate Nehru as a "reactionary nationalist."[20] Khrushchev's willingness to withdraw his missiles from Cuba without insisting on an American no-invasion pledge on Castro's behalf may have suggested to the Chinese a similar willingness to abandon them in a pinch; on November 5, the *People's Daily* hurled its famous charge that the Soviet Union was trying to "play the Munich scheme against the Cuban people."[21] The infuriated Russians promptly withdrew their support for the Chinese in the Sino-Indian border dispute[22] and, after some hesitation, began to sell large quantities of arms to the Indians.[23] In December Khrushchev rebuked the Chinese, though not by name, for their policy during the Cuban crisis and taunted them for not having dared to "liberate" Hong Kong and Macao.[24] In short, in a matter of the greatest concern to China, Khrushchev had supported Nehru against Mao; and in a crisis threatening the survival of the Soviet Union, Mao had supported Castro against Khrushchev.

Under the circumstances, the Chinese stood virtually no chance of rejuvenating the Sino-Soviet alliance or blocking the badly shaken Khrushchev's moves toward détente

---

[20] "More on Nehru's Philosophy in the Light of the Sino-Indian Boundary Question," *People's Daily,* October 27, 1962.

[21] "The Fearless Cuban People are the Most Powerful Strategic Weapon," *People's Daily,* November 5, 1962. The Chinese also seem to have incited the Cubans to obstruct the removal of the missiles and bombers.

[22] "Negotiations Are the Road to Settling the Conflict," *Pravda,* November 5, 1962.

[23] Indian Defense Minister Y. B. Chavan announced in May, 1964, that up to that time the Soviet Union had sold or agreed to sell $130 million worth of such arms to India (*The New York Times,* May 13, 1964). For Chinese objections to Soviet Indian policy, see "The Truth About How the Leaders of the CPSU Have Allied Themselves with India Against China," *People's Daily,* November 1, 1963.

[24] Report to the Supreme Soviet, December 12, 1962. The Chinese responded by threatening to review the treaties that had fixed the Sino-Russian border in the nineteenth century ("A Comment on the Statement of the CPUSA," *People's Daily,* March 8, 1963).

with the United States. They could only hope that Kozlov
and his supporters would check Khrushchev or perhaps
even overthrow him. But early in May, 1963, it was announced in Moscow, without details, that Kozlov was ill,
and nothing has been heard of him since. Soviet jamming
of the Voice of America was soon reduced and then
stopped entirely on June 18. Already the Chinese had
warned Khrushchev [25] not to sign a test-ban treaty, and
they seem to have retained a hope that he would not almost until the actual initialing of the treaty on July 25.

The test-ban treaty was a traumatic event to the
Chinese, as it was to de Gaulle.[26] The treaty tended to obstruct the nuclear ambitions of both, not so much in a technological sense as in two political ways: by dealing with a
matter of great concern to them without their participation
or consent, and by creating an "illusion of peace" (a Chinese
term) in which atmospheric testing even by a non-signa-
tory would create an adverse world-wide reaction.

The current phase of Communist China's foreign policy
dates from the test-ban treaty and is designed to compensate for and exploit a Soviet-American détente that the
Chinese apparently consider too firm, at least for the time
being and with respect to matters threatening the security of
both superpowers, to be disrupted. The Chinese are probably afraid of further Soviet-American "Munichs" at their
expense, such as an agreement on a "two Chinas" policy,
and perhaps even of an explicit Soviet abandonment of
them to the United States.

The Chinese answer has been to attempt a unique and
difficult kind of third-force policy. Communist China is

[25] By implication, in their letter of June 14 to the Soviet party's
Central Committee, four days after President Kennedy's speech at
American University, in which he had indicated willingness to sign a
treaty banning all but underground nuclear testing.

[26] For de Gaulle's statement on the treaty, see *The New York Times,*
July 30, 1963. The Chinese position was conveyed in statements of
August 15 and September 1, 1963.

trying to create, with itself in the pivotal position in both, two coalitions based on a platform of anti-Americanism and anti-Sovietism. One coalition, corresponding to the revolutionary or party aspect of China's dual policy, is a species of "international" composed of Communist parties, newly constituted "Marxist-Leninist" splinter parties, and front organizations that show some willingness to follow Peking's lead.[27] The other coalition, corresponding to the national or state aspect of Chinese policy, centers on a so-called "third world" composed of China itself, France, West Germany, Britain ("on the condition that she ceases to be a courtier of America," according to Mao Tse-tung), Japan, and Italy.[28] The economic inducements to China to improve its relations with the industrial powers are obvious, but there may well be a military motive as well. The Chinese may hope to improve their military position and compensate for the virtual collapse of the Sino-Soviet alliance by aligning themselves with France[29] and perhaps even with West Germany[30] and Sweden.[31] The Chinese also hope to contribute to splitting the Western countries and Japan from the United States politically, mainly through the lure of trade and secondarily through crude devices such as the assertion that the United States is try-

---

[27] For the Chinese rationale of this process, see Chou Yang, "The Fighting Task Confronting Workers in Philosophy and the Social Sciences" (delivered October 26, 1963; published by the New China News Agency on December 26, 1963, Mao Tse-tung's seventieth birthday).

[28] Based on Mao's statement to a French delegation (*The New York Times*, February 21, 1964).

[29] Thorez has recently referred to the "de facto agreement between de Gaulle and Mao Tse-tung about the dissemination of the nuclear weapon" (quoted in *The Washington Post and Times Herald*, March 29, 1964).

[30] The East Germans have recently accused the Chinese of seeking a *rapprochement* with West Germany at their expense (*The New York Times*, April 25 and May 15, 1964).

[31] A Chinese military delegation visited Sweden in the autumn of 1963.

ing to "enslave" them. The Soviet Union has charged in
alarm and anger that the Chinese are exaggerating the
"contradictions" between the United States and the other
"imperialist" countries and are whitewashing the latter,
West Germany in particular.[32]

At the party, as distinct from the state, level of their
dual policy, the Chinese have continued to seek support
from extreme militants in the Western Communist parties,
as against the Soviet Union, as well as to maintain a degree of pressure on the Western governments, by demand-
ing the liberation of the remaining Western colonies,
denouncing the allegedly continuing "neocolonialism" of
the West in its former colonies, and advocating militant
struggle by the local Communist parties rather than purely
parliamentary maneuvering, in part as a means of com-
batting Western colonialism and "neocolonialism" in the
underdeveloped areas.[33]

At the time of writing, it seems entirely possible that the
Soviet-American détente and the worsening of the Sino-
Soviet dispute may have an effect on Chinese domestic
policy no less dramatic than its effect on Chinese foreign
policy. In its New Year's editorial for 1964, published five
days after Mao Tse-tung's seventieth birthday, the
People's Daily announced that "politics is the commander
and soul" and urged that "the whole nation should learn
from the experience of the People's Liberation Army,
which has a splendid tradition in political work [34]—slogans
remarkably reminiscent of the "Great Leap Forward" of
1958-60. They have given rise to what appears to be an

---

[32] Cf. Suslov's report to the Soviet party's Central Committee, "On
the CPSU's Struggle for Cohesion of the International Communist
Movement," February 14, 1964 (note the anniversary of the Sino-
Soviet alliance), published on April 3.

[33] "The Proletarian Revolution and Khrushchev's Revisionism,"
People's Daily and *Red Flag,* March 31, 1964.

[34] "Advance from Victory to New Victory," *People's Daily,* January 1,
1964. See also "The Whole Country Must Learn from the People's
Liberation Army," *People's Daily,* February 1, 1964.

effort to militarize public life, and economic life in particular, to an extent unprecedented in China.[35] In February, 1964, Po I-po, a leading Chinese economic planner, said that after China finishes repaying its debt to the Soviet Union in 1965, it will launch another major industrial investment program.[36] Such a program, in a country that is only just recovering from the "Great Leap Forward" and whose leaders preach the virtues of national self-reliance, would presumably mean a further intensification of pressures on the unfortunate peasants.

Implications for the West

The tendency toward a détente between the Soviet Union and the West, which has been especially pronounced since the Cuban missile crisis, has been advantageous to the West, in the sense that it has reduced the chances of a general war. On the other hand, the atmosphere of détente has enhanced Soviet political attractiveness in many areas, including some Western countries, and has tended to foreclose certain opportunities for creative Western statesmanship that were present in the Stalinist period. Furthermore, there is no denying the strong probability that the

[35] "Benefiting from the socialist education movement and learning from the PLA and other advanced units on a large scale, the workers, peasants, and other working people of the country since the beginning of this year have unfolded the movement for increasing production and practicing economy in the form of comparing with, learning from, and catching up with the advanced and helping those lagging behind and have achieved great results. During the course of the movement, many people have freed themselves from their old thoughts, gained broad viewpoints, and learned other's experience with an open mind. The valuable experience, good work style, and proper measures of the advanced units and individuals are being disseminated quickly and becoming the common assets of the society" ("Carry Out in a More Practical Manner the 'Compare, Learn, Overtake, and Help' Campaign for Higher Production and Economy in Celebration of May 1, International Workers Day," *People's Daily*, May 1, 1964).

[36] *The New York Times*, February 7, 1964.

Soviet Union's motives in seeking détente have been to a large extent tactical and opportunistic in nature. The Soviet leadership has of course been moved by a general fear of nuclear war. More specifically, it is very likely that Stalin's successors were appalled by the way in which Communist China's refusal to sign an armistice in Korea until all Chinese prisoners of war had been repatriated, coupled with Stalin's apparent willingness to threaten the United States in support of the Chinese, had created a serious risk of nuclear war in the Far East and even of general war by the time of Stalin's death in 1953.[37] If this is so, it follows that Sino-Soviet differences, in particular over questions of Communist China's national interest as the Chinese define it, have contributed to the Soviet-Western détente, as the latter has in turn contributed to the worsening of Sino-Soviet relations. The process seems to have had the character of a self-reinforcing cycle. To argue that the Soviet-Western détente is a good thing because it has produced a deterioration of Sino-Soviet relations would be to oversimplify.

Furthermore, it is far from clear that the Sino-Soviet dispute is entirely a good thing for the West. It is, in the sense that it is easier to deal with two opponents if they are divided than if they are united, and both the Soviet Union and Communist China remain fundamentally opponents of the West. On the other hand, just as the mutually reinforcing phenomena of Soviet-Western détente and the Sino-Soviet dispute have tended to increase Soviet attractiveness, so they have tended to increase certain forms of Chinese pressure on the non-Communist world. With trade as the main bait and with the hope of isolating the United States from its friends and allies, Communist

---

[37] On the Chinese attitude see Chow Ching-wen, *Ten Years of Storm* (New York: Holt, Rinehart and Winston, 1960), p. 82. On Stalin's attitude, see K. P. S. Menon, *The Flying Troika* (London: Oxford University Press, 1963), pp. 26–29.

China is wooing the non-Communist industrial countries; for the latter to play the Chinese game without risking a Chinese victory over themselves as well as over the United States would be possible, but not easy. The development of the Soviet-Western détente has also seen a great increase in Chinese national and revolutionary activity in the underdeveloped areas, clearly to the disadvantage of all Western interests and not merely those of the United States. The Sino-Soviet dispute has rendered the Soviet Union virtually unable to restrain this activity, should it feel inclined to do so.

Probably the main reason for Chinese militancy at the revolutionary, as distinct from the national, level is a desire to maintain the validity and momentum of the Chinese model of Communist-led, anti-imperialist revolution in the underdeveloped areas by means of a major victory in the near future. South Vietnam would be the most desirable scene of such a victory from the Chinese standpoint, even though the North Vietnamese, who are under Chinese influence but are by no means a Chinese satellite, would be the main beneficiaries. Conversely, the absence of a Communist victory in South Vietnam would constitute a major setback to Chinese ambitions for ultimate hegemony in Asia and for the export of the Chinese model of revolution to the underdeveloped areas as a whole. It would seem to be a matter of great urgency for the West and for the non-Communist world in general, and not only for the United States, to prevent such a Communist victory in South Vietnam. Neutralization would mean, as it is apparently coming to mean in Laos, to concede the area to the Communists by degrees and without a struggle. The slogan of neutralization for South Vietnam was advanced by the North Vietnamese through their South Vietnamese agents, and endorsed by the Chinese, in 1962, a year before it was officially espoused by France.

Although Chinese revolutionary militancy is generally

conceded, there is a fairly widespread feeling in the West that this militancy can be restrained, or even eliminated, by injecting the spirit of détente, unilaterally if necessary, into the relations between China and the West. This hopeful view overlooks the fact that Britain, India, and the Soviet Union have already tried to restrain Chinese militancy through conciliation and have failed. What has been most effective in restraining Communist China, apart from the political desire not to shock world opinion excessively or unnecessarily, has been the military power of the United States and the Chinese estimate of American willingness to use that power against China if sufficiently provoked. To alter this syndrome would require more than conciliation by the West. It would probably require a change of leadership in China drastic enough to produce a major change of policy. Such a shift is a possibility, but by no means a foregone conclusion, after the death of Mao Tse-tung. Such a shift also seems more likely to be induced by a Chinese belief in Western unity and firmness than by a belief in Western disunity and softness.

Finally, it makes little sense for the West to sympathize in any active way with the Soviet Union in its controversy with China, whether for ethnic reasons or because of lesser Soviet militancy. The Soviet Union is a threat to the West of a different order from China, but it remains a threat. In a military and economic sense, it is obviously by far the greater threat. The Western statesman contemplating the busts of Khrushchev and Mao might reasonably murmur, may the worst man lose.

The Risks of a Détente Policy to Central Europe

by

Alfons Dalma *

The optimism with which this last period of relative détente has been viewed in broad circles of the West is understandable but at the same time surprising. It is not difficult to understand that prosperous democratic society, by its nature and philosophy, considers a permanent conflict as alien to common sense and therefore only too easily believes that the opponent, too, must one day realize the senselessness of the Cold War. But it is astonishing that this instinctive optimism of the West ignores, far too easily, several fundamental and critical factors: namely, that the last four years of the Eisenhower Administration and the first two years of the Kennedy era were characterized by the utmost sharpness in the permanent West-East conflict;

---

* *Alfons Dalma:* German and Austrian political writer, foreign affairs columnist for *Die Presse* (Vienna) and *Münchner Merkur* (Munich); editor, defense policy review *Wehrkunde* (Munich); teaches political strategy in Munich High School of Political Sciences; author of *The Backgrounds of the Berlin Crisis* (Karlsruhe, 1962) and *De Gaulle, Germans, Europe* (Karlsruhe, 1963).

that the phenomenon of Soviet détente policy—as in earlier days—always starts with the expectation that the West will make concessions without Moscow having to make a similar contribution to the settlement of the conflict; and finally that even the last period of the so-called détente was not free from aggressive efforts of the Communist powers, China as well as the Soviet Union, as expressed for example in the continuation of the Soviet's Cuban policy, the air incidents over German territory, the efforts of the Soviets to take advantage of the Cyprus crisis, and the intervention in the Indo-Chinese affair in favor of the Vietcong partisans.

The sudden pitch of highly critical danger, and the settlement of the crisis during the Soviet-American Cuban conflict in October 1962 dramatized vividly the transition from brinkmanship to détente. A few months later this impression of détente between the West and East was strengthened by the conclusion of the Atomic Test-Ban Agreement. The continued and for the most part confidential contacts between the Soviet and the American governments, which have not been interrupted since the Cuban conflict, help considerably to spread the impression that the East-West conflict is on the point of settlement.

Nineteen of the last twenty years have been characterized by tension, by a world-wide conflict of interests, and by the so-called Cold War between East and West. This struggle for world-strategic decisions between the Soviet Union and the United States of America, and their respective bloc and alliance systems, has been pursued with all means, except all-out world war, and actually began during the last months of World War II against Hitler's Germany. It has not always been carried through with the same intensity. Between the high points of the first Berlin crisis, the Korean War, the events of the year of 1956, the second Berlin crisis and the Cuba crisis, there have been periods of summit and other conferences, armistice negotiations, and agreements between the protagonists of the Cold War. Throughout the nineteen years, however, no one has doubted, neither in the East nor in the West, that the conflict was a permanent one and that it had to last until such time as its origins—the international expansionist aims of Soviet policy and the unsettled problems left by World War II in Europe, in Asia, and in Africa—had been removed. However, for approximately one year now the conviction seems to have gained ground in the Western world that in place of the Cold War a period of détente has begun.

The difficulty in analyzing the détente in Central Europe and its results lies in this inability to explain the phenomenon. After all, just what is détente? Certainly, as a word and a concept it has been launched by the Soviet Union. But in the experimental attempt to make it into a policy, it has been taken over by the United States. Allies of the two superpowers have tried to orient themselves accordingly. London, Bonn, and Rome support the efforts of Washington. Warsaw, Budapest, and Belgrade, Bucharest and Sofia, and recently Prague, have followed the directives of the Soviet détente strategy. To be sure, for China and France, this period was the occasion to criticize Moscow and Washington and to free themselves to a great extent either from the solidarity of the Eastern bloc system or from the Western alliance. But this makes the material contents of the period of détente neither clearer nor more tangible. At best one can say that the policy of détente is characterized by the willingness, or by the ostensible readiness of the nuclear great powers (through permanent and confidential diplomatic contacts as well as through minor empirical adjustments), to alleviate to some small degree the dangerous character of a status quo loaded with incendiary problems and, always, to defuse the conflict when they fear they are losing control over developments. The admitted motives behind this policy are first the fear of slipping into a nuclear war, and second the efforts of the established nuclear powers to prevent the proliferation of nuclear weapons or, at least, to keep them under control. This is no small feat even though it does not constitute anything new and has been in effect even in times of greatest tension and crisis. But it is surely too little on which to base a détente for settling the conflict.

The Détente and Central Europe

Another difficulty of the analysis is the concept of Central Europe. When there was still a homogeneous Europe, prior to the Soviet conquest of the East, Central Europe included Germany, Austria, and Switzerland, as well as the belt of the countries between the Baltic Sea and the Adriatic Sea: Poland, Czechoslovakia, Hungary, and at least western Yugoslavia. Since 1945 the Soviet power system in Europe has separated one-half of Germany and the entire zone between the Baltic and the Adriatic from Central Europe and has made it an integral part of East Europe. The shifting of the center of Western political power to America had the effect that only western European peripheral areas—the British Islands, Spain and Portugal, the Scandinavian states—can be regarded as the modern Western Europe, in so far as they tend more to the West than to Europe. "Central Europe" has also shifted westward: it has become western European, continental, and, at the same time, free from and immediately endangered by Eastern Europe. These are the countries of the European Common Market—the Federal Republic of Germany, France, Italy, and the Benelux countries—as well as, from the geographical viewpoint, the neutral countries of Austria and Switzerland.

Still, we cannot limit the definition of Central Europe to this, if the importance and the effects of the détente with respect to this area are to be examined. The separation of the states between the Baltic and the Adriatic from Central Europe was one of the causes of the permanent tension. With regard to their history, culture, and—even today—their economy and their way of living, the peoples of Poland, Czechoslovakia, Hungary, and Yugoslavia strive toward their reincorporation into the Central European territory. A genuine détente, therefore, would also have to include these countries and in this way restore the homogeneity of the area with regard to economic and cultural relations and freedom of movement of traffic and persons. The Central Europe of the Cold War lies westward from the Iron Curtain and stretches to the channel, the Gulf of Biscay, the Pyrenees and the Tyrrhenian Sea. The Central Europe resulting from a genuine détente should be extended to the East to the line of the eastern boundary of Poland, Czechoslovakia, Hungary, and Yugoslavia, that is, up to a vertical north-south line, Koenigsberg-Ragusa.

The attempt alone to define the concepts is perplexing. Either one expects under détente an organic and peaceful new arrangement in Europe—and if this is the case then up to now there has been no détente; or the détente is an attempt to come to terms with and adjust to an unorganic and unorganized European status quo—if this is the case it is artificial, misleading, and is not of long duration.

It is a weakness of the academic spirit to employ firm concepts where the reality consists of vague terms; to want to operate with scientifically fixed entities where experimental uncertainties must be employed in a political equation. Détente is more a hope than a policy. However, it suffices already that it is a hope and a slogan in order to make it into an element of reality. In the past it was not easy to determine the borders and the characteristics of Central Europe, and today it is more difficult than ever and will not become easier when an attempt is made to sketch a picture of the future. And yet the concept of a Central Europe is a practical political necessity. Despite the vagueness in the concept it is certain that there is a Central Europe, that a strategy of détente makes it into a field of experiment, and that a whole series of world-wide Central European problems will be drawn into this experiment of détente: the security of the West, the continuation of the Atlantic Alliance in its European sphere, the political and economic unity of Europe, the fate of the present satellite states, the question of drawing boundaries in Central Europe and—first of all and in its entirety—the German question and/or the problem of the German division, which, nobody can deny it, will be of "pivotal importance" for the future of East-West relations. An examination of the effects of the détente experiment thus far, in these categories of political problems, should reveal whether or not the détente, up to now, has been a successful strategy of the East and an error of the West.

Western Security in Central Europe

This should be an axiom: Europe is an essential element for the security of the entire West and for the United States. Platitudes may be banal, but they are inevitable in a methodical analysis. The entire modern history of Great Britain for over four hundred years started from this understanding and was characterized by a policy of security which successively was directed against the hegemonic claims of the old House of Austria, of France, Russia, and modern Germany. Since then there has been no change in the basic conditional factors. Of the former continental hegemonic powers only one is still in existence, but this one, Russia, is more powerful than ever. The principal liberal world and sea power of the West is no longer Great Britain, but—farther across the ocean—the

United States of America. Today, all former European great powers and all free European minor states, as a consequence of the shift of power in favor of the Soviet Union and the United States, are the allies of America. NATO is the manifestation and the instrument of this Western policy of security.

The Western world, from San Francisco to Athens, looks upon itself as a homogeneous unit because of its historical development, its cultural-historical community, its religious, ethical, and social-philosophical principles. Nevertheless, within this homogeneous area, which is supported by mutual security interests, fundamental differences resulting from history and geography also exist.

The Western world consists of two different parts, of Europe and of America. Europe is a subordinated unit within the Western community. But it is again in its internal structure extremely differentiated. History has created a variety of nations and states in an area of very different geographical conditions. European unity, therefore, is a necessity and a goal, but is not an automatic conclusion. From the standpoint of Western security, however, it is indispensable. A Europe that lapses back into its historical discords would be neither a useful partner in the world-wide American policy of security nor an effective barrier against Soviet expansion. It would also not be an economic-political unit in the dimensions of the modern world.

Since policy, however, is not only rational planning but is also subjected to the impluses of history, tradition, customs, and particular interests, the inner cohesion of Europe does not depend so much upon recognizing a common political philosophy, but rather upon two practical factors and influences: the continued support of America and the threat of the Soviet Union. If one or the other influence subsides, Europe runs the danger of falling back into the particularism of its past, and of putting current national interests ahead of common European and Western interests. The so-called détente awakens illusions which have effects precisely in this sense. It permits the impression that the threatening danger from the Soviet Union is abating, and it conveys the impression that the United States of America is more interested in a settlement with the Soviet Union than in the unification of Europe and in an organic settlement between such a Europe and America.

As a matter of fact, the originators of Western détente strategy have discovered as their method the so-called policy of movement. In so doing they unintentionally slipped into the role of a magician's apprentice, and they seem to have lost control over their own invention. If the U.S. and Great Britain deduce from the principle of flexibility the right for themselves to pursue détente goals with the Soviet Union, they can hardly prevent their European partners, among themselves and in their external relations from "getting into motion." As a result, the cohesion of the Atlantic Alliance and of Europe must suffer. It could have been anticipated that General de Gaulle would practice a policy of movement of his own. It should not be surprising that the German Federal Republic sees in the American détente strategy aspects of insecurity against which she tries to reinsure herself by special relations with Paris. It is natural that Italian politicians adapt the American policy of movement to the demands of their domestic politics and that they use it as a device to realize the "opening to the left" which makes Italy in foreign policy a dubious NATO member and leads her toward neutralism. Under the conditions of détente euphoria, it is normal that the opposition in Great Britain, Germany, and France feel encouraged, independent of American concepts and indeed far beyond them, to replace a security policy with new variations of the old pacifistic ideologies of European socialism. Also, it is not surprising, in connection with a policy of détente, that French and Italian democratic socialists seem again to find advantage in co-operating with the Communists on domestic policies, and in re-establishing popular fronts. If Washington finds that Moscow, although it maintains the status quo in Europe and the world, can be an honorable partner for partial agreements without a basic reform of the status quo, then it is only logical that European left-wing democrats again start to look upon Communists as acceptable partners for restricted operations in domestic affairs. The first con-sequence of détente, which to date is more a challenge than a practical reality, manifests itself in a general loosening in the political unity of European states and in the domestic discipline of European leftist parties vis-à-vis Communist offers for co-operation.

That means diplomatic gains for the Soviet Union and tactical advantages for the Communist parties. These suc-cesses of the Eastern détente strategy in Europe have not been matched on the Western side by equal gains through a policy of movement at the expense of the strength or inner cohesion of the East bloc, a point which has yet to be demonstrated.

When the late President Kennedy announced his "New Frontier" program, Europeans could well understand that with it he wanted to proclaim new goals for the develop-ment of American society and to broaden old horizons. The old American spirit of the frontier and of the pioneers thus has been transferred from its former geographical setting into the social-political sphere. But some Europeans had to ask themselves whether their American friends realized the revolutionary change within the Western world, which has actually reversed the concept of "border." The Amer-ican pioneers have carried the Western border of occidental culture and civilization, during one of the greatest epochs of humanity, to the shores of the Pacific Ocean. But since the world-wide power demands of Russia and the strange civilizing claims of world communism have torn Europe into two halves, the words "border," "border spirit," and "pioneerdom" of the Western world have changed direction. The geographical, political, and cultural "New Frontier" of the Atlantic world today is located at its Eastern periphery, in Europe.

What has been accomplished here in order to establish, to extend, and to consolidate this border against the Communist East can well be compared with the miraculous activity of the American pioneer, at first in the Middle West, and then in the Far West of America: the revival from the ruins of World War II, certainly through American help, but also through long years of privation and obstinate work by the Europeans; the overcoming of a thousand years of dissension; the enthusiasm of the youth for a united Europe; the creation of a Common Market, in keeping with needs of the century, for almost 200 million persons; the rebuilding of a common military defense establishment on the earlier battlefields of the European nations. This modern Europe fulfills its function within the West, in which it is buoyed by a new "border spirit," a new "spirit of the frontier." As in the American pioneer period, this spirit is on the one hand conditioned by a determination to create a better world and a more just order, and on the other by a consciousness of a permanent danger which threatens this work from the other side of the border. If, however, one gives it too much weight, then the so-called détente strategy could weaken these two impulses. If the West views the Soviet Union and the Communists as appropriate and willing détente partners, then they and their political and social order appear neither dangerous nor bad.

The détente philosophy seems to shake the foundation of Western security. Even if we disregard the fact that in all probability there can be no modest settlement through limited détente agreements between the Soviet imperialist claims and the Communist order on the one side and the

Western international order and system of society on the other side, there still remains the following basic understanding of modern security policy: the effectiveness of the deterrent strategy and with it the maintenance of world, if not local, peace depends on both a complicated and simple balance of nuclear and conventional armament and defense preparedness in East and West. In other words, to live securely in the atomic age means the willingness and the ability to live dangerously. The enthusiasm for a détente policy endangers, one-sidedly and to the disadvantage of the West, the knowledge of the Western peoples of this necessity and the readiness of free men to guarantee their security by a willingness to risk their lives. A détente policy has therefore this remarkable aspect which especially in old Europe shows questionable effects: it awakens illusions that one can master the demands of a modern security policy in the atomic age with methods and political customs of the nineteenth century, the demands of the conflict-laden mass age with recipes of the "cabinet politics" of the "ancien régime." It blunts the dynamism of the internal development and the external appearance of the West. This would be perhaps no misfortune if the same effect would also take place in the East. Up to now, however, this has not been established. It may not be accepted as a matter of course, because the mechanism of Communist society and the Communist ruling system is free from such "spontaneous" reactions to "atmospheric" changes in international politics. There is in the East no free play of psychological forces, but only a planned-in-advance policy of a relatively very small, uniform, and solid circle with clear-cut person-and-group interests.

The Relaxed Alliance

The Central Europe of today has in the Atlantic Alliance the indispensable political and strategic backbone, the foundation of its security. Lying in the foreground of the Soviet political and military organizational sphere, it possesses neither space nor people nor sufficient power to guarantee its security with its own resources. Moreover, this Central Europe lacked, until the beginning of the French nuclear armament, every starting point for development toward a nuclear power, while the Soviet Union is one of the two super, atomic powers. Politically and strategically Central Europe is dependent upon the Alliance with the United States and with Great Britain, as well as on the depth of the Iberian peninsula (in order to gain space in depth). As long as there is an East-West opposition and as long as, even in peacetime, the Soviet Union remains a towering superpower, the Atlantic Alliance is the fate of Central Europe.

Within the Atlantic Alliance, the other pillar of the European position in the world, opposing the Eastern bloc, and in the dimension of the modern economic and industrial society, is a united Europe whose best and most progressive expression thus far is the European Economic Community. In contrast, the political unity of Europe has developed only to a limited extent. Since France and Germany are by far the two strongest and most important continental powers, the French-German Treaty nevertheless represents a starting point toward Europe's political unity.

NATO, EEC, and the special French-German relations are, therefore, three pillars upon which the security, the world position, the prosperity, and the political unity of Central Europe rest. The policy of détente has thus far, again as a matter of fact, perceptibly weakened all three pillars without having contributed anything toward the stability and security of the situation. That is a staggering balance.

This détente policy, which is, in principle, difficult to define, has, in fact, many and obvious aspects. There are three aspects of the policy which have a particularly negative effect upon the cohesiveness of the Atlantic Alliance: (1) the continued American-Soviet talks which are surrounded by secrecy; (2) the display of a certain nuclear-strategic solidarity between the United States and the Soviet Union; and (3) finally, the relaxing of principles upon which the Western policy with regard to Germany had thus far been based.

1. The continued bilateral contact on the diplomatic level between Washington and Moscow, which has assumed an almost institutional character, started with the exchange of secret letters between President Kennedy and Premier Khrushchev. Reportedly it is also continuing under President Johnson. It resulted from the second Berlin crisis and from the Cuban crisis, and the American government was practically forced into it by Moscow. As it is, this in itself did not make a good impression everywhere in Europe. The fact that it was bilateral and secret was all the more bound to create the impression that the U. S. government was giving way to Soviet pressure and was seeking détente in bilateral discussions which, in view of the uncompromising Soviet attitude, could only mean that the U.S. was asjusting to the demands from Moscow.

Reactions on the European continent varied from state to state, but in one respect they all had the same effect: the relaxing of Alliance discipline and new demands on the part of the most important European Alliance partners. Since France is the most independent of all European states, possesses the greatest freedom of action, and has a strong and stable government, its reaction was the most violent. This chapter of de Gaulle's policy is known: the demand for the right of co-decision in world politics and, in Alliance strategy, the employment of a highly individual and independent French policy within the Alliance and in East-West relations. This French attitude can be reduced to a simple formula: in the same degree to which Washington shaped its East-West policy as a political strategy of movement and flexibility in East-West relations, Paris replies with its own policy of motion and flexibility. This was considered a heavy blow against the inner unity of the Western Alliance in Central Europe. At the same time, however, the Central Europeans were impressed that the French "policy of aloofness"—as compared with American détente strategy—in meeting Soviet policy, particularly in Europe, was much firmer in adhering to former, common Alliance principles. This created, for instance in Germany, the impression of an unpleasant alternative. The defense of Germany's political interests seemed to be in better hands with de Gaulle than with Kennedy, while there was no change in the belief that the interests of German security and that of all of Central Europe could only be taken care of by the power and defense willingness of the United States. This is no real alternative, no real choice, because there can be no choice between the interests of political and defense policies. The act of balancing between Paris and Washington, to which the continental states have since been forced is, however, a far too unsteady political ground upon which to base an effective and stable alliance structure.

The exclusive bilateral talks between Washington and Moscow have, in the eyes of Europeans, given only too well the semblance of legitimacy to one of de Gaulle's central theses. It is the thesis according to which Europe should have more power and independence in representing its interests, because these interests might not always and under all circumstances be entirely identical with those of the United States. The appeal of this doctrine, which is furthered by the détente policy, is able to damage the Alliance severely, as long as it is not either refuted or, in agreement with the U.S., accepted as an integral principle of the Alliance. (The same thesis, by the way, can be found in the analysis of the nuclear-strategic aspects of détente.)

2. In the same way in which the nature of "détente" can-

not be concretely defined, so its manifestations too are difficult to define. The most evident manifestations are the negative effects upon the inner unity and the power potential of the West. This is especially true of the nuclear-strategic aspects of the détente policy.

The visible expression of the détente policy in the nuclear field is the Moscow "test-ban" agreement. It is, in itself, insignificant. It does not limit nuclear armament, it does not prevent the further expansion of the nuclear potential of the Soviet Union and the United States. Nor can it prevent the proliferation of nuclear weapons, because the only two powers which are presently attempting to become atomic powers, France and China, have not acceded to the Moscow treaty. That this test-ban treaty was, nevertheless, presented to the world as a great achievement of the policy of détente, both by the governments of the United States and of the Soviet Union, the attention of politicians and analysts was drawn away from the modest contents of the treaty, and the general interest concentrated on the philosophy from which the treaty springs and upon possible hidden factors. It is generally concluded from the Moscow agreement and from the attitude Washington and Moscow take in their nuclear policy that there is a tacit agreement between the Soviet Union and the United States to keep the club of atomic powers exclusive; that in the event a major world war threatened to break out a certain solidarity between the nuclear superpowers would take precedence over any other obligations, and the powers would settle any major crisis first of all through negotiations among themselves and without their allies. This would, of course, also mean that the two atomic superpowers consider it their prerogative in the event of a military conflict—in Europe for instance—not only to keep as their own exclusive right the determination of time, scope, and intensity of employing nuclear weapons, but also to make this the topic of bilateral discussions and contacts. This would be the diplomatic equivalent of the strategic doctrine of flexibility which is called the McNamara doctrine.

Such ideas give rise to a whole series of misgivings and apprehensions in Central Europe. One considers this a success of the Soviet cold-war strategy of the policy of pressure and blackmail. Experts in the European chancelleries analyze the evolution of the past years and determine that the American nuclear-strategic flexibility theories have been developed and officially adopted in the same degree in which the long-standing Berlin crisis, with its alternating high points, forced the responsible Americans to review all possible risks involved in a conflict over Berlin. It has not escaped Europeans how quickly the Moscow test-ban treaty followed upon the climax of the Cuban crisis with its display of nuclear power on both sides.

This evolution suggests the conclusion that a bold handling of their nuclear weapon potential for the purposes of political blackmail enabled the Soviet Union to force the United States into a nuclear strategy and policy which is separating America and Europe, causing distrust between the allies and paralyzing the military development of the Western allies.

As a result, in the eyes of Europeans, the United States has suffered a loss of prestige. Rather than acting as the superior nuclear superpower to deter the Soviet Union, the United States has shown rather too much, it is believed, how sensitively it reacted to the intimidating power of the Soviet Union. So sensitive in fact that, for the sake of a tacit, standstill agreement with Moscow, the United States would mortgage their relations with the most important and oldest allies, disregard the principle of equality within the Atlantic Alliance, and subject the once indivisible security of Central Europe by adopting a mobile and elastic scale of strategic deterrent concepts.

There is a whole catalogue of European misgivings against the nuclear-strategic aspects of such a détente.

Each one of these reservations is a political reality, which brings with it practical disadvantages for the Alliance.

The principle of exclusiveness in the atomic club cannot, in the long run, be accepted by the European powers or it will lead to a paralysis of the defense will in Europe. (*a*) It contains elements of inequality, even though the United States and the Soviet Union seemingly treat their allies on the basis of equality. And (*b*) it leads the Central Europeans, via the detour of the policy of nuclear disengagement in Central Europe, to consider conventional defense preparations as senseless.

a) Like Great Britain, which has stubbornly insisted on the necessity of its own small nuclear potential, so France cannot accept being placed by the United States on the same level with the East bloc countries, and Communist regimes like Poland or Czechoslovakia. In Germany and in defense-conscious circles of Italy this is not voiced as loudly as in France, but they think it. If the Soviet Union expects and demands of the United States that the U.S. should treat her European allies and potential nuclear powers in the same way as Moscow treats its satellite states, then the Soviet government, with the semblance of equality is in fact deliberately playing a very unequal game. Great Britain, France, Germany, and Italy are allied states of a dimension of power and of a political system for which there is no parallel in the Soviet satellite area. Poland, Czechoslovakia, Rumania, and Hungary are neither technically capable, nor power-politically able to carry even a fraction of the responsibility for their military security. Formally they are allies of the Soviet Union; militarily and strategically, however, they are merely provinces or colonies of the Soviet imperium, and at the most can be called upon to provide auxiliary troops. This is different in the West.

While the United States is by far the superior military and economic power in the Atlantic Alliance, Great Britain, France, Germany, and Italy (and far more so a politically united Europe) represent political and military factors which have their own function within the Alliance. In attack and in defense the East bloc practically means only the Soviet Union. No defense is conceivable in Western Europe, if even one of the great powers of Europe would not fulfill its military and political function. Therefore, if the Soviet Union should succeed in forcing the United States to treat her European allies, in such an important field of politics and strategy as the domain of nuclear weapons and their distribution, as Moscow treats its East European satellites, then Khrushchev would have induced the Americans into applying a principle to the Western Alliance which does not correspond with its nature. The same principle is adapted to the structure of Communist control in Eastern Europe. In Western Europe it must have a disintegrating effect upon the unity of the Alliance.

There is another circumstance which makes equal nuclear-political treatment of Eastern and Western Europe absurd. It is the difference in the danger. Eastern Europe is not constantly endangered by the West, but, rather, it is the other way around. This is not without bearing on the distribution of the nuclear deterrent or on the conduct of war. Germany and consequently also France are the constant objectives of a systematic Soviet strategy of blackmail. The Berlin crisis alone has shown this. Central Europe, therefore, is vitally interested in a strategy of nuclear deterrence down to the smallest detail, including the stationing of nuclear weapons in Germany, the co-decision and co-responsibility in determining nuclear defense strategy, the targeting and operational orders; perhaps even in the co-possession or possession of nuclear weapons. A satellite state, as for instance Poland or Czechoslovakia, however, has never in the past nineteen years been threatened by the West, not even politically, much less to speak of political pressure and blackmail based on arms and nuclear weapons. To conceive of détente, therefore, as a policy which would make the control over strategic nuclear weapons exclusively a preserve of the Soviet Union and the United States, would mean for Central Europe a diminution in her security and in the effectiveness of her deterrent strategy, while the security of the satellite states, which are an integrated part of the Soviet power, would remain unaffected.

b) This aspect of détente policy may result in different consequences in Europe, under contrasting signs. For France it means justification of her efforts for strategic nuclear autonomy. For a Conservative Great Britain the prospect of a Soviet-American nuclear monopoly is a reason to concentrate its armaments on its own atomic force; for a Labor-governed England the temptation is strong to associate itself with pacifistic ideas, in order, with the assistance of the doctrine of disengagement, to avoid any nuclear responsibility, and also to reduce conventional defenses to a mere formality, meaningless in the atomic age. On the Italian political scene such a policy of détente furthers the influence of neutralist left-wing socialists; in their eyes—and not unjustifiably—nuclear disengagement in Central Europe would mean a half neutralization; and once strategic nuclear responsibility would be set aside, Italy's readiness for defense with conventional weapons would soon totally dwindle away. Admittedly, a maximum will for defense exists in the Federal Republic, but belief is very weak in the usefulness of a force which, although Europe's greatest conventional army, would have no part in sharing the responsibility for the nuclear deterrent and strategy. The readiness of Germans to maintain and to reinforce a large conventional army is based on the expectancy that these armed forces will also be prepared for atomic warfare, that German territory by the presence of heavy nuclear weapons inside the German boundaries will continue to be earmarked as a part of the Western "sanctuary," and that Germany will, in some form, actively participate in control of the Western nuclear command structure, as well as in the planning of Western nuclear strategy. The nuclear aspects of détente policy raise doubts as to whether such expectancies will be fulfilled. They therefore perplex the Germans. On one side they further inclinations to look for a solution by a political and military union with France, on the other side they further the temptation to strive for a neutralization of Germany via disengagement, especially since many Germans cultivate the hope that neutralization might possibly gain Soviet agreement for reunification. A continuation of the policy of détente, with all its present political and military unclarities, might completely disorient the Germans within several years, though during fourteen years of the era of Adenauer they have been the most consistent and faithful partner of the United States within the framework of the Atlantic Alliance.

3. With a policy of détente more than defense preparedness is at stake in Germany. One who knows the early history of German rearmament realizes how difficult it has been to bring Germans to accept it. For one thing, they still suffered from the shock of the Hitler period and defeat in World War II; secondly, there existed a widespread opinion that rearmament and joining NATO barred chances for the re-establishment of German unity. Détente, with the maintenance of the status quo, therefore, would not only give Germans the belief that the continued existence of a large conventional army would be meaningless, but it would also stimulate the desire to seek reunification, at least in stages, by gradually coming to terms with Soviet conditions. If a few years before the termination of the North Atlantic Treaty Alliance a détente favors such tendencies as well as activates de Gaulle's efforts for an autonomous foreign policy and strategy, then it represents an extremely critical development for Western unity and for American world policy.

The German question is the European main-piece of the East-West relationship. The consequences of détente policy on the German situation, therefore, may be of real political-strategic significance. It is necessary to analyze them in a special section. Even more than in other fields détente in Germany threatens more than in other areas to "relax" the Western Alliance to the point of dissolution.

The German Incertitudes

The period of détente of the year of 1963 is, as has already been stated, a consequence of a four-year-long acute crisis in Berlin, and of a short, but violent crisis in Cuba. Whether this relaxation of tensions has facilitated, simplified, and brought nearer a solution of the United States' Cuban and Latin American troubles is not the subject of this analysis, but it seems doubtful. But at the end of this analysis it is established that a détente has neither changed the facts of the German problem nor improved the chances of the West German policy. The unclarities of a policy of slogans—détente, flexibility, movement—seem already to have resulted in the beginning of a critical disorientation, partially in a relapse into ideas which had already been overcome, of a German alternative to NATO policies, to the U. S. alliance and to the united Europe, and to a revival of old German incertitudes.

An analysis of the effects of détente policy on Germany deserves special attention. The German question is a key problem of East-West relations. The Soviets know very well in what perspective it must be seen. The December 27, 1961, memorandum of the Soviet government addressed to the Federal Republic begins: "The Soviet Union and the Federal Republic of Germany are the most important states of Europe. . . ." That is one of the starting points of Soviet German policy. The other is illustrated by Khrushchev's speech in Leipzig on March 7, 1959, a key text of great significance, which demonstrates basic Soviet planning not only for the Berlin crisis of the years 1958 to 1962, but also Soviet détente policy of the year of 1963:

> We support Germany's reunification, and the German people will be reunified. This is only a question of time. However it is decisive, on which basis it will be reunified. . . . The West Germans will one day understand that it would not be so bad to have Walter Ulbricht as Federal Chancellor and Otto Grotewohl as President of a reunified German Peoples' Republic. . . . If the people of Western Germany are not yet ready to accept it, then one should not hurry too much. Provisionally two states may exist. . . . As one says: Everything in its time. . . .

Earlier, during a period of acute crisis, and during a delicate East-West balance between truce and open war, the United States and the West have understood perfectly Moscow's strategy for Germany. Christian Herter, then Secretary of State, reported on the collapse of the Geneva Foreign Ministers' conference during the summer of 1959 on American television as follows:

> The Soviets did not give any indication that they are interested in genuine negotiations. They engaged in much propaganda. . . . Once again they have shown that they are not willing to use normal methods for regulating international affairs. It has been demonstrated that it is their long range goal to keep Germany divided until the time has come for the establishment of a single German state under Communist influence. To hasten the achievement of this goal, the Soviets strive for the integration of West Berlin into the Communist power bloc. All their Berlin proposals are designed to bring them closer to this goal. The acceptance of the Soviet proposals would lead to an important retreat by the West through which the

world would learn the lesson, that the Soviet Union
is the dominating power in this part of Europe. . . .

Looked at in this context Soviet détente policy in Germany appears to be a variant of Russian strategy for
the conquest of Germany. The direct threat of force
and the handling of the Berlin crisis brought fewer advantages to the Soviet strategy on Germany than détente tactics, with which the West—mainly the U.S. and Great
Britain—seemingly co-operate. Extortion by power gal-
vanized German resistance; the atmosphere of détente,
which seems to cement the status quo, discourages Germans because it gives the impression that the national
future of Germany and its national unity depend solely and
exclusively on an arrangement between Moscow and the
Germans.

The virulent four-year Berlin crisis ended in Western
Germany the old dispute between Konrad Adenauer's
Western orientation and socialist policy of reunification (on
a neutralist tangent). Since 1960 the two large German
parties have apparently supported the same policy of a consistent Western orientation, which made the still existing
"Eastern" inclinations of the National Liberals insignificant. Toward the end of 1963 this situation began slightly
but significantly to change again. This is a consequence of
the atmosphere of détente.

The change polarizes itself around the contrast between
Berlin and Bonn. A typical Soviet détente maneuver has
helped to reawaken the old opposition between Christian
Democrats and Social Democrats. This was the offer
to issue passes to West Berliners for visits to East Berlin
at Christmas, 1963. This step carried little risk for Ulbricht
and Khrushchev, since the function of the Berlin wall remained untouched. It was a characteristic détente gesture
which did not cost the East a thing but which might
bring the East gains in the West. The advantage for the

East was that the Lord Mayor of West Berlin, Willy Brandt, accepted the offer and that German Federal Chancellor Erhard, though reluctantly, still gave his conditional consent to this idea. Thereafter West Berlin stepped forward as an independent bargaining partner of the Ulbricht regime, entirely in the sense of the Soviet demand for recognition of West Berlin as an independent state. The consequences could be seen in February and March, 1964, when the Lord Mayor of West Berlin, who in the meantime had been elected chairman of the Western German Social Democratic Party, wanted to continue negotiations for visitors' passes with the East Berlin regime on the basis of the Christmas precedent, in contrast to the government in Bonn and to the official attitude of the three Western allied powers. Suddenly the bipolarization of German policies between Bonn and West Berlin, and the old foreign policy differences between the foreign policy of Konrad Adenauer, which Erhard has taken over, and the efforts of the foreign policy opposition, the Social Democrats and the Free Democrats, became visible. This is a significant result for an inexpensive détente gesture by the East. But it is also the doubtful result of the Western tendency to acquiesce in the détente tactics of the East. It is no secret that West Berlin's Lord Mayor and the Chairman of the Social Democratic Party in Germany, Willy Brandt, is determined to adapt his pass policy in line with Washington's intentions, as a part of the much talked-about "policy of movement." Washington's détente tendencies are apparently sufficient to convince some German politicians to adapt such a "policy of movement" in Berlin and in Germany.

As a consequence of the détente atmosphere, nothing tragic or irreparable has yet happened in Germany. The Social Democratic reorientation in the question of the pass negotiations is only a beginning, a temptation to return to the neutral or neutralistic foreign and German policy of the nineteen-fifties. But in such an unstable situation as that of a divided country, even symptoms must be tested carefully. Even more significant than the temptations of the Social Democrats have been the reactions of the national liberal Free Democrats. Encouraged by Willy Brandt's uncertainty, the most active foreign political speaker of the liberals, Thomas Dehler, has again started to propagate a policy of direct and bilateral contacts, negotiations, and arrangements with Moscow; and of direct talks between Germans and Soviets, not withstanding the disappointing results of his own talks with Khrushchev.

On the one side, therefore, the détente atmosphere furthers German illusions of a bilateral understanding with Moscow. As the pass negotiations show, such a policy is enough to bring the Soviets closer to the prerequisite for their plan for Germany's conquest, namely to the fixation of the status quo. If American détente policy gives the impression that it tacitly agrees with such developments in Germany, it can only strengthen such tendencies among the opposition in foreign policy. And on the other side, those German forces, which always formed the "party of the West," the camp of the followers of NATO and of the U.S. alliance, will be tempted to look for the support of France and de Gaulle in order to preserve the former German policy of the West.

To sum up the consequences of détente policy introduced by the East and pursued or at least tolerated by the West: in Germany it raises doubts as to the usefulness of defense efforts and the strategic-nuclear guarantee of security; it gives the impression of cementing German partition and it leads to a temptation to overcome this crucial issue of German national politics by direct talks with the East; it furthers the inclination to seek reinsurance against abandonment of German national goals by Washington by turning to Paris and de Gaulle's "all-European" neutralism of a third force. Furthered by détente, in Germany both tendencies—(1) reunification on the basis of neutralism through an arrangement between the Germans and the Soviets; and (2) reunification on the basis of neutralism through an arrangement between the Soviet Union and a Europe of a "Third Force" located between America and Russia—are not compatible with the real foundations of security and freedom of Germany and Europe, as well as with the security of the U.S. Viewed in the perspective of the German circumstances, détente reveals itself as a dangerous and not ineffective tactic and weapon of Soviet cold war strategy.

Détente Without Countergain for the West in the East

In so far as there exists in the West a serious theory of détente strategy, it is based on a broad view of the development of Eastern society. W. W. Rostow is doubtless right in observing signs of fatigue in the system of Communist domination, world unity, and economy. The centrifugal forces in world communism, the demands and needs of life and economy in individual Communist states, including the Soviet Union, may foreshadow a development, at the end of which Communist powers may exist which place more value on security and prosperity than on expansion and conquest. A policy of détente in such a perspective would be a logical means to further liberal developments in the Communist East, by releasing Communists from their fear of the West. For this fear is considered an element inhibiting the hoped-for development of centrifugal forces and the aspirations of prosperity and security.

Logical in theory and supported in many practical manifestations, such a détente doctrine encounters three unclarified factors:

1. It cannot be predicted in which time period this development of Communist society will be accomplished and whether it will proceed linearly or dialectically with relapses into aggressiveness and imperialism.

2. It is an open question, because it has not been factually determined, whether the Communist powers may be or must be afraid of the West, including the Germans.

3. It is possible that Communist power holders and ruling classes are more afraid of the natural evolution of their society in the direction of liberalization than they are of the West.

Even if Western détente tactics should be the right answer for a determinate natural development of Communist society, certain disadvantages of the détente atmosphere in the Western camp must be accepted. It is therefore important to ascertain what consequences détente has in the East.

Soviet world and foreign policy has not changed basically as a result of détente. The demands of the Soviets in Europe and Asia have remained the same. Their position in Cuba is still, as it has been in the past, the starting point for a long-range subversive policy in Latin America. Their subversive activity in Africa continues. Notwithstanding the informal economic crisis in Russia, assistance, greater in relative terms than that of the U.S. and Western Europe, is being given for these purposes. A return to open methods of terror and pressure is always possible. Even during Stalin's time there were changing phases of tension and détente. This alternation of methods characterizes the whole Khrushchev era. And even if Khrushchev himself has completely departed from the strategy of crises and fixed his policies on a détente strategy, the play of internal political forces within the power sphere of Soviet ruling classes leaves open all possibilities for change. That would devoid Western détente tactics for the furthering of liberalizing tendencies within the Soviet Union, of any character of a truly effective grand strategy. Its justification and chances depend on the initiative of the Soviets and on the vicissitudes of Soviet policy.

This would be a minor inconvenience if the political-strategical machinery of the United States and Western Europe would be as elastic and polyvalent as the Soviet-Communist. The Soviet power apparatus is in a position not only to switch nearly automatically and directly from détente to tension, but also to play simultaneously the two varieties of the world political strategy. The Western system cannot do so. The necessity to prove any phase of political strategy before the public, to get the agreement of public opinion and of the Allies, who in turn must win their respective public opinion—all this introduces into the flexibility of Western politics a considerable amount of inertia. There is something basically contradictory in the theoretical attempt to undertake to tie a powerful but ponderous democracy to a policy of movement. Possibly this is one of the reasons why the Soviet apparatus wants to take the cold war out of the trenches and onto the field of movement. The Kremlin would then have the advantage. In any case it must be stated that, notwithstanding détente policy, the Soviet power apparatus remains intact and operationally active for the employment of tension and crisis strategy, while our analysis indicates signs of paralysis and dissolution in the West.

This picture does not change essentially when one analyzes the European satellite sphere of the Soviets. Western strategists anticipated that détente would produce or at least further certain signs of independence from Moscow in the satellites' foreign policy toward the West and with regard to the main East-West issues. The opposite must be reported. Thus far the greatest loosening in the ties of dependence has taken place during periods of the most acute East-West crises. Tito's defection occurred at the time of the first Berlin crisis. In contrast thus far, the greatest *rapprochement* between Moscow and Belgrade has taken place during the periods of détente in the years 1957 and 1963. The move toward Polish independence and Gomulka's coming into power occurred during the crisis year 1956. They appear to be Soviet concessions in the face of a threatening danger of world conflict; the same is true of the original relaxation in Hungary, which then led to the Hungarian freedom uprising. However, these same two countries, during the détente atmosphere of the last twelve months, submitted in greater degree to Soviet foreign policy, and the Communist leadership achieved a stronger concentration of power, political control, and discipline.

Within the Warsaw Pact area and its military organization, that is, as concerns the character of total satellite military dependence on Soviet Russia and the complete military entity of Eastern Europe, absolutely nothing has been changed through détente. Evidently the Soviet army insures with an iron hand that the military organization of the East bloc remains completely untouched by the ups and downs of Khrushchev's tactics of tension and détente. This picture is—as has been demonstrated—in crass contrast to the disintegrating consequences of détente within the military and defense sphere of the Atlantic Alliance. Again the same picture results: through détente the Soviets win advantages in the West, without suffering disadvantages in their own area. The reverse—no gains in the East, disadvantages in their own area—has thus far been the détente balance in Central Europe for the West.

There exists another plausible explanation for this situation, in addition to the relatively greater political-strategical flexibility of the Communist apparatus as compared with the immobility of the democratic system. This other explanation is possibly even more important. Free society and a free coalition or confederation of peoples and states are always pulled this and that way between the knowledge of their mutual interests and the immediate and popular impulse to emphasize national and local interests rather than the abstract common and supranational interests. Under such circumstances, a too extensive détente, by removing the visible outside danger, almost automatically results in a relaxation of the West. In the East it is different, because the rulers in the Soviet Union and European satellite states, which do not have the size and self-assertion of China, are tied together by a primary common interest. This is stronger than national and local interests. This fact has been mentioned here already: the possibility that the Communist ruling groups may be more afraid of liberalizing tendencies within their own countries than they are of dangers from a continued tension between East and West.

For the Communist ruling class there is a security limit to the relaxation of tensions externally and internally, a limit to all concessions to internal prosperity and to the easing of world problems. It is the limit of the exclusive maintenance of power by a very small ruling minority. Even for a Tito or a Gomulka the exclusive maintenance of power and privileges by the Communist apparatus is more important than the national independence of Yugoslavia and Poland or the internal satisfaction of the Poles or the South Slavic peoples. This was demonstrated in November, 1956, by Belgrade's recognition of Ulbricht's regime and by rupture with Bonn in 1957. It is just this undemocratic character of the satellite governments that is the hardest cement of the unity of the East European bloc. Up to now no strategy of détente by the West has been able to shake profoundly this solidarity. This makes its "dynamism" and "offensive character" more than questionable.

Concluding Remarks

The balance in Central Europe is negative after three years of American policy of flexibility and one year of Western policy of détente. This policy has increased the

internal tensions of the Western Alliance. It has dulled
the sense of the Eastern danger and the need for Western
defense preparedness. It has, in the area of Eastern and
nuclear policy, increasingly placed before Europeans, and
not just in Germany, the false alternatives of Kennedy or
de Gaulle, Washington or Paris. It has revived ideas of
disengagement not only in Great Britain, but also on the
continent, although these are the first step to an active
neutralism. It is about to reawaken in Germany the old
dichotomy—Western alliance or reunification with the help
of the East. As NATO is entering the last five years of its
actual treaty, that is the last quarter of its existence which
is assured by the treaty, the détente is promoting centrifugal forces and exclusively national orientations. One
could say: two more years of such a policy of détente and
the remaining three years until 1969 will not be sufficient
time to reunite the Atlantic Alliance, to bring the
Alliance partners together, and thus to preserve NATO
until the end of the century.

For the East bloc, on the other hand, the détente period
of the last years has proven a relief. It has enabled Moscow to honorably camouflage its defeats in Berlin and Cuba.
It has completely checked the effects of these reverses. It
has allowed Khrushchev time to attend to Russia's internal
political and economic problems and even to receive Western assistance. It appears to have led to tighter discipline
within the East bloc.

In fact, the détente of 1963 was only an admission of the
inability of Moscow to make progress in the German area
and Latin America by the use of force in Berlin and Cuba.
In the West, on the other hand, there was understandable
relief that there was not greater misfortune in either Berlin or Cuba. The relief appears to have been so great that
the West in its euphoria has forgotten that it has not been
rescued in Germany and Cuba through Russian good will,
but rather because it has won two real victories in the Cold

War. While the Soviet Union has utilized this relief to further its détente strategy, the Soviet Union has prevented the West from utilizing the effects and strategic amplifications of its victories.

This analysis, so the author believes, sticks to the facts. It may give the impression of condemning a Western policy of détente while praising the efficiency of an Eastern détente strategy. In reality it proceeds from the fact that détente is a neutral political-strategic concept. A détente policy can just as well be good as bad. It depends on the results it achieves. If up to now it seems to have brought the West nothing but disadvantages—and not only in Central Europe—then the policy was either employed at the wrong time or not handled correctly. Probably the major weakness to be found in Western détente policy is its defensive and static character. The democratic powers seem to expect nothing more from their dynamic and still aggressive opponent than a static insistence on the conditions of the present situation. With an unstable and explosive status quo such as exists today not only in Europe but also in Latin America, Africa, and Asia, détente means that the West gives to the dynamism and expansive desires of the East practically a free field. This phenomenon is perhaps more apparent and visible in Central Europe, especially in Germany, than elsewhere.

Toward Stability
in Central Europe

by

*James E. King, Jr.**

I

The post-World War II unity of the West became a pre-occupation, and a phrase to conjure with, in an international context that no longer obtains. It was based, moreover, on a premise that has proved to be no more than half true. The international context was the challenge of what then appeared to be a monolithic and vigorously expansionist Communist East, dominated by the Soviet Union. To this challenge the West responded by uniting to accept the support and leadership of the United States, which abandoned its drift back to isolation to rearm and reentangle itself in Europe's affairs. The premise was an assessment of the intentions of the Communist leaders, specifically of Joseph Stalin, who was believed to be determined not only to employ the surge of domestic communism in other countries—reinforcing it with the intimidating image of Soviet military power—to exploit the debility, internal

---

* *James E. King, Jr.:* Senior Research Associate, Institute for Defense Analyses, Washington, D. C., and Research Consultant, The Johns Hopkins University Washington Center of Foreign Policy Research.

disorder, and loss of confidence of the non-Communist world, but also quite literally to advance the Communist cause by military aggression.

The invasion of the Republic of South Korea by Stalin's satellite regime in North Korea in July, 1952, was judged proof of the Communist belligerent intention; this was particularly disturbing to Western Europe because it appeared to supply a plausible explanation for the armed forces the Soviet Union was then engaged in building up in East Germany and in the satellites of Eastern Europe. As a consequence of this judgment, the military arm of the North Atlantic Treaty Organization—originally conceived as a West European defense supported and guaranteed by the United States—became a North Atlantic military command structure (incorporating substantial force contributions from the United States and pledged to the rearmament of the West Germans) which undertook to build in Europe a defense able to contain and defeat a surprise attack by vastly superior forces from the East.

The cold-war context has lately been altered. It has been altered, above all, by the disarray into which the East has fallen. This disarray was foreshadowed by the disaffection of Yugoslavia as early as 1948, but has only lately become unmistakable in the Sino-Soviet dispute and other signs of the concessions that empire and ideology have had to make to nationalism. As one especially striking feature of the familial feuds, the group of Communist parties still led by the Communist party of the Soviet Union has given new focus and meaning to the necessity of "peaceful coexistence" and has sought to lay the ghost of the persistent if perhaps questionably legitimate dogma that, in the Marxist-Leninist view of things, an ultimate war between the socialist and capitalist "camps" is inevitable.[1] At the

---

[1] See Frederick S. Burin, "The Communist Doctrine of the Inevitability of War," *American Political Science Review*, LVII, No. 2. (June, 1963), pp. 334–54.

same time, in consequence of its own recovery and the diminished sense of threat from the East, the West has been experiencing its own transformation and evolving its own polycentrism, which has called into question the willingness of Europe to respond to United States leadership except in the event of a renewed menace from the East.

Meanwhile, the oversimplification of the West's judgment of Communist military aggressiveness has been exhibited, not just in what the Communist leaders have said over the years—which was properly regarded as suspect—but in the military power they have provided themselves. The interaction of their programs and the West's has produced what can accurately be described, though not as a "balance" of all capabilities, as a global "balance of imbalances." A great United States superiority in intercontinental strategic power (against which, however, the Soviet Union maintains an intercontinental minimum deterrent that is conceded effective) is opposed to a correspondingly great Soviet superiority in strategic power on the continent of Europe (against which of course the strategic power of the United States counts as a "minimum" deterrent). Accompanying this asymmetrical balancing of the long-range nuclear advantages, the armed confrontation on the ground in Central Europe, both in conventional forces and in terms of battlefield nuclear weapons, more nearly approaches a military balance of the familiar order. The standing forces of the West are stronger than their immediate opposition and are better supplied with tactical nuclear weapons, but they are less uniform in staffing and equipment, their command is less effectively integrated, their logistics probably more vulnerable, and their reserves both less numerous and in a lesser state of readiness.

Though the balance-of-imbalances has produced a military equilibrium of sorts, often thought of as a "nuclear stalemate," it is less stable—more war prone—than comfort demands. The reasons for this are both political and military, though perhaps more the former than the latter. The principal reason is that at a number of points, and notably in Central Europe with which this account is concerned, the East-West confrontation involves unresolved conflicts of vital interests that are in a state of merely suspended hostilities.

This state has two major characteristics. The first is the determination on both sides to use all available means, including military force, to preserve existing positions. Thus neither side will permit the other to achieve the solution to which it is pledged. The second characteristic is that both sides are also determined to keep open, by every means available, including military force, the possibility of influencing the eventual settlement and, thereby, of achieving the solution to which it is pledged.

This means that each adversary is alert for signs of weakness of the other. It means further, however, that each tends to present the other with an image of aggresiveness that, in moments of acute crisis, raises the imminent threat that one of the two will panic or miscalculate the other's intention. On the NATO side, as will later appear, the diagnosis of the threat and the agreed requirement for forces to meet it have produced a military posture that is less appropriate to a protracted cold war than to imminent hot war, and still less to the context in which East-West relations have lately been moving toward a more relaxed status. The posture of the East appears less immediately warlike, the privilege perhaps of having seized the political initiative earlier.

This being the case, the confrontation in Central Europe is not, as it might otherwise be, a balance of latent strength in which the opposing military forces cancel each other. If it were, the threat of military action would sink into the background leaving the foreground to political relations and diplomatic maneuver. It is, rather, a flawed military deadlock which has in it the potentiality of action initiated by one side or the other regardless of the predictably disastrous consequences to both. This potentiality becomes apparent every time the local conflict stirs from its suspended animation and, worse still, may do so even when the actual point of contest is outside Central Europe. Thus the most disturbing feature of the Cuban crisis of the fall of 1962 was the ready acceptance of the idea that the Russians might be tempted to compensate themselves for their loss of face in Havana, where they were militarily weak, by turning the screws on Berlin, where (or so they had been told often enough by the West) they were correspondingly superior.

Because of the recalcitrance and the extreme gravity of the issues, the crises of the Cold War come promptly to focus on Central Europe. The chief issue is the contest over Germany's future. In the past the West's problem was to resist Russian efforts to exploit the exposure of West Berlin as a means of extorting recognition of East Germany and therefore of the legitimacy of Germany's partition. Now that the Russians, as a consequence both of their growing appreciation of thermonuclear destruction and of their problems in the bloc, favor détente, the unresolved question of Germany stands in the way of movement toward new political and military relations that are more durable and reliable.

In brief, despite recent, fundamental changes in the conditions that determined the character of East-West relations, the general effect of which is to blunt the sharp edge of conflict, the confrontation in Europe and specifically in Central Europe, remains unstable. This continued instability has been traced to two sets of circumstances, one relating to Germany, the other to the military security problems of non-Communist Europe. There are no more significant questions for United States foreign policy than those in which these situations give rise. The two subjects are obviously interrelated and consequently cannot be treated in isolation one from the other. It is possible, nevertheless, to examine them separately, and this will be done in the next two sections of this discussion, taking the problem of Germany first.

II

As differences over German occupation policy were the immediate occasion for the breakdown of the coalition that was victorious in World War II, so it was inevitable that the future of Germany should be a primary source of East-West conflict in the postwar era. Soviet policy on Germany has been a mixture of negative and positive elements, of determination to punish, humiliate, and exploit the Germans—making certain they remain too weak to express their resentment—and of efforts to recruit the whole German people as willing or unwilling members of the socialist camp. When both campaigns failed and Occupied Germany was divided into Western and Eastern parts, it became Soviet policy to hold out the hope of unification as the means of frustrating the effort of the three Western powers to sponsor West Germany's economic recovery and to bring about its orderly reincorporation in the community of European states.

This endeavor also ended in failure. The record of the Soviet Union in dealing with Eastern Europe, highlighted by the brutal subversion of the Czech Republic, had taught the West, and the German people, to mistrust its initiatives. The United States, in particular, was disabused of its postwar hope for a collective security system based upon collaboration in the United Nations, and in time recommitted itself to the security of Western Europe, an essential feature of which was the decision to arm the West Germans. The latter accepted the decision and with it acquired a sense of acute dependence upon the strength and will of the United States for support against the Soviets.

Though this decision was made in 1950, actual rearming was delayed by the fiasco of the European Defense Community, and the first German soldier did not don his uniform until 1956. Nonetheless, the conclusion was accepted by the Soviet Union when the Federal Republic joined NATO in 1954. From that time forward, Soviet policy, which at the last moment had professed itself willing to accept a united Germany that was neutral and guaranteed by a European Security Pact, if it could not have a Communist one, appeared no longer to be interested in reunification but rather in extorting recognition of the permanent disunity of Germany.[2]

In the meantime, of course, through all the changes of policy and prospect to which they were subjected, the German people have never ceased to desire and demand reunion. In accepting association with a West European defense arrangement supported by the United States, the West German leaders realized full well that they were abandoning any early hope of achieving reunification by direct negotiation with the Soviet Union or by playing West against East. Nevertheless, the decision did not mean they were forfeiting hope. Some may have associated the rupture of unity and Communist dominance of East Germany with the relative decline into which the non-Communist world had permitted its military power to fall. These looked for an eventual favorable settlement, and for German reunification in freedom from communism, after the West had recovered its strength. The many who were partisans of a united Europe possibly believed that the road to German reunification would be opened through the progress of Western Europe toward a new unity—a unity that would so

---

[2] The best summary discussion of these early postwar developments is found in Alastair Buchan and Philip Windsor, *Arms and Stability in Europe* (London: Chatto & Windus, 1963), Chapter II, pp. 24–50.

absorb Germany that the old terror of the Germans would cease to obsess Eastern Europe. It may also be assumed that many West Germans were persuaded, as were many Americans, of the forecast associated with the United States policy of containment, namely, either that a transformation of the Soviet Union or its waning relative strength would in time cause it to release East Germany.

Events have not taken any of these courses. Though the Soviet Union has experienced domestic instability, and is doubtless facing it again in the succession to Khrushchev, it exhibits few signs either of disintegration or of basic accommodation to Western values. Further, though in some respects its military power has declined relatively, as the West in NATO has made up the neglect of the immediate postwar years, the achievement and exploitation of nuclear military power by the Soviet Union have so mitigated the effects of this decline that hopes for benefits from it have turned out to be quite unfounded.

What has in fact occurred to alter the context of German unification are the changes in other directions, note of which was taken in the first section to this essay. As was stated there, the changed relations within and between East and West, despite notable effects upon the prevailing atmosphere, have not brought political nor military stability to Europe. The German issue is still unresolved and still subject to crisis renewal, either at the option of the Soviet Union, and perhaps even of the Communist regime in East Germany, or in consequence of the impact of heightened tensions outside of Europe, as in the Cuban crisis of 1962.

The key to this instability, from the West's point of view, is the future of East Germany. If there is to be any basic stabilization, any lessening of the ultimate peril that exists despite changed East-West relations, that improvement must be found in Germany itself. Meanwhile, because of the more equable environment, the German confrontation has become less acute. Perhaps because of this some long-term amelioration is also possible. To examine that possibility requires a look at East Germany and at inter-German relations.

In this discussion little if anything need be said about Berlin, which, in many another context, would hold the center of attention. The reason is that Berlin, though an immensely difficult problem for the West while East-West relations remain unfriendly, is symbol and consequence, not cause, of that unfriendliness. If the changed relations of West and East Germany that are examined below as possibilities should come about, the Berlin problem would abate. Eventually, it is to be hoped, it would survive only as an administrative headache, to be finally cured in the amicable if distant reunion of the German peoples.

Since August, 1961, when the Berlin Wall put an end to the drainage of productive manpower, the East German regime has been stable, though at an unimpressive, even if improving, level of vitality. Meanwhile, the evolution of the East European Communist regimes in their varied directions has made the German Democratic Republic of Walter Ulbricht an anomaly—the only one that still looks and, by and large, behaves like a Soviet satellite.[3]

Moreover, aside from Hungary, where the remains of a suppressed rebellion are still being tidied up, East Germany is also the only Communist-controlled territory in East Europe still occupied by Russian troops (if we count the two Soviet divisions in Poland as line-of-communication troops for the German occupation). Twenty Soviet divisions are assigned to the Warsaw Pact command, and there is no question that one of their roles is to "defend" East German territory against NATO and West Germany. There is also no question, however, that another of their roles, which they have practiced successfully in the past, is to

---

[3] Even in Bulgaria there have been autonomist stirrings. *New York Times,* May 17, 1963; July 21, 1963.

dominate the East German population, which is the best measure of Ulbricht's stature as a Communist leader.

Nevertheless, Ulbricht has won a degree of autonomy from the Kremlin. This is indicated by some of his actions, which appear to be out of step with current Moscow moves. Presumably his proven ability to survive crises, such as those of June, 1953, and the Wall, has made him too valuable a Russian asset to be handled roughly.[4] Anyway, he does still survive, even though what he stands for contrasts so unfavorably with the growing acceptance of the Communist regimes in Eastern Europe that it must sometimes be a source of embarrassment to Khrushchev.

As an example both of Ulbricht's independence and the fact that his position sometimes embarrasses the Soviet Union, it may be noted that since the Berlin crisis that began in 1958 has been allowed to subside, Khrushchev has played down the issue of the West's recognition of the East German government. Not to have done so would hardly have been compatible with his interest in détente. He has not, however, been followed in this by Walter Ulbricht. Specifically, it is believed by some close observers that the initiative for the Christmas passes, permitting West Berliners to visit relatives in East Berlin in December of 1963, came from Moscow. There is no question, however, that Ulbricht ran the venture and exploited it by all the means available to him to try to gain some degree of recognition.

Since they gave up offering unification in hopes of blocking West German rearmament in 1954, the Russians have made the issue of the recognition of East Germany the touchstone of the West's acceptance of their policy of two Germanys. Thus the presence or absence of Soviet persistence on the issue of recognition has served to measure

---

[4] The story is told that, in reply to a question about Ulbricht by a West German visitor, Krushchev recited the parallel of the Russian peasant who, annoyed by his son, suddenly realizes that, at eighteen, the latter has become too old to be slapped down.

the intensity of the Cold War in Central Europe. Likewise, the insistence of the East German government on recognition has become one of its marks of identification, and the fact that Ulbricht continues to press the issue when the Kremlin is not doing so may indicate some independence on his part.[5]

If there is any chance that Ulbricht has indeed become an embarrassment to the Soviets, it is worth considering whether Khrushchev may sooner or later undertake to change the image of the East German regime. Probably the more conservative judgment is that he will continue with his Hamlet's choice of supporting Ulbricht for the time being. Some alternative cannot, however, be entirely ruled out. In any case, Ulbricht cannot last forever. Persistent rumors regarding his ill health suggest that if he were to be invalided to the Black Sea coast it would not necessarily be for purely political reasons. It is, therefore, appropriate that the West should be examining the alternatives available to Khrushchev and should be considering how its interests might be affected by them.

How would Ulbricht be replaced? One possibility is that his successor would be as like him as possible, only more responsive to Soviet discipline. Even so, some degree of internal relaxation and some effort to improve the outward impression of the regime would be in keeping with the trend in Eastern Europe, and therefore seems probable.[6]

Would the Russians dare to permit the East European relaxation to be extended to East Germany? If they did,

---

[5] It will, of course, only indicate the subtlety of Khrushchev's tactics of détente—to anyone who can think of Khrushchev as subtle.

[6] The favored Ulbricht-like successor is said to be Erich Honecker, a party secretary who made his reputation as organizer of the Communist youth in East Germany. Now in his early fifties, Honecker has served as stand-in for Ulbricht on some recent ceremonial occasions. Another possibility is Willy Stopf, recently acting prime minister, whom some regard as less rigid than Ulbricht. He is the latter's contemporary, however, and seems to lack both the vigor and the standing in the party likely to be expected of the successor.

how far would they mean to go and by what means would they expect to be able to stop the evolution once it is started? Khrushchev himself is surely under no illusions regarding the risks involved. If either of the parts of Germany ever swallows up the other, without forced feeding from the outside, it will not be the seventeen million who ingest the fifty-six million, nor the unpopular ideological East German regime, dependent on alien bayonets, that comes to dominate the popular government of the Federal Republic. If such indications as are at hand mean the Russians do favor change affecting East Germany, there must be some explanation for it beyond the minimal desire for a regime less isolated by the changes in Eastern Europe. Two possible kinds of explanation appear to be worthy of consideration.

Khrushchev may believe he can bring about a controlled relaxation in East Germany that will further dim the image of "threat" from the East, thereby contributing substantially to the disarray of NATO. He might expect to accomplish this by first spurring internal dissension in the Federal Republic, as indeed he has already succeeded in doing to some degree. If this is his purpose, he no doubt expects this dissension to communicate itself to NATO and to the relations between the United States and its allies in NATO. This explanation is consistent with the thesis that the détente in East-West relations is exclusively the result of Soviet tactics. It is also, however, consistent with the possibility that Khrushchev is employing the tactics of détente to make the best of changes in East-West relations he has neither created nor been able to control.

The reason why it might be attractive to Khrushchev to extend the détente to relations between East and West Germany is that the major consequence of renewing pressure on West Berlin, or reviving the campaign for the recognition of the East German government, is, as he must be fully aware by this time, to give NATO renewed vigor and to confirm the unity of the West. So long as it was possible for Khrushchev to suppose he might bludgeon the West into acknowledging the permanent division of Germany, there was reason to believe he would not consider reviving NATO too high a price to pay. By now, however, even he must be prepared to recognize that this campaign has failed. To stimulate NATO to no good purpose seems unlikely to be attractive to him. At the moment at least, the détente must appear more promising. He must already have seen evidence of its success in encouraging NATO's increasing disarray. It is suggested, therefore, that if Khrushchev considers it can be done without running undue risks of losing control there, he might be happy to see East Germany change from a goad to the West's unity into a source of contention disruptive of that unity.

There is, however, another kind of possibility. Given the whole complex of the issues involved in his personal and official position, including the emphasis he has laid upon gains to be made by the Soviet Union in an atmosphere of improved understanding with the United States, the attention he is forced to give the Sino-Soviet contest over leadership of world communism, and his acceptance (thus far) of the polycentric and autonomist trends in Eastern Europe, it is conceivable that Khrushchev has an entirely different objective in mind. It no doubt would reflect a changed conception of the future of Central Europe, one more compatible with "peaceful coexistence" and improved relations with the United States. Progress down this road could not go very far without indicating that the time had come to think of withdrawing Soviet forces from East Germany and abandoning the Communist regime there.

The possibility that such a policy of *rapprochement* with the West is Khrushchev's objective is thus far sheer speculation. Perhaps such a sharp departure from past policies will come only if growing enmity between the Soviet Union and Communist China makes it imperative that the Soviet front to the West be pacified. It would be absurd to take it for granted that this is the direction in which Khrushchev proposes to go. At the same time, it would hardly seem necessary or wise for the West to put obstacles in his way if it turns out that something like this is in his mind.

For whatever reasons, however, some kind of change in East Germany—in line with, even though lagging behind, the changes in Eastern Europe—appears likely. It is objected by those who argue that the experience of East Europe is unlikely to be repeated in East Germany, that nationalism cannot supply the motive for autonomy in a fragment of a country. They also maintain that an intensely unpopular regime is unlikely to risk liberalization. Perhaps this is true of Ulbricht himself, who is too old to change anyway. The regime that replaces Ulbricht, however, may not be so unpopular initially and, by adopting policies recognized by the East Germans as being intended to improve their condition, it may be able to capitalize popular interests even though it cannot enlist nationalist sentiment.

The regime that instituted such a policy line could hardly be a fanatic one. Nor is it likely to be the instrument of another Old Communist such as Ulbricht. It might, however, as the Kadar regime seems to have done with success in Hungary, attain the status of a sort of Communist caretaker.

The West Germans conceive of their relations with East Germany in terms of three distinct patterns of thought. The first is the legalistic pattern, which is commonly stressed in public statements by the Bonn government. In accordance with this pattern there is pedantic insistence upon the importance of the way the East German issue is handled. The nominal justification for this is the need to avoid precedents that will lead to *de facto* recognition of East Germany.

As is usually true in such cases, however, there are underlying substantive issues. These are, first, to make sure that no government gets the idea that the West German government is relaxing its claim on East Germany and, second, that none of the allies of the Federal Republic, particularly the United States, is relaxing its support of the Federal Republic in asserting its claim. The same legalism, directed outwardly, justifies the Hallstein Doctrine (by which the Federal Republic withholds or withdraws diplomatic relations with any government—except the Soviet Union—that recognizes the East German government). It explains also why the U.S.-Soviet talks have been so closely scrutinized and, on occasion, so harshly criticized in Bonn.

The second pattern of thinking about West-East German relations is represented by the insistence of the West German government that the East German regime lacks real autonomy and must, therefore, be regarded as an agent of the Soviet government. As the Federal Republic considers itself unable to deal effectively with the Soviet Union on a matter of such vital importance, this view of course adds to the Federal Republic's dependence on the United States. The necessity of West German relations with East Germany, at the very least on problems of access to Berlin but also in connection with trade between the two parts of the country, and the insistence of both governments that Ulbricht is significant mainly as an agent of Moscow, have combined to require the closest intimacy between the U.S. and West German governments whenever a new problem involving inter-German relations arises.

When these two patterns are combined, in the fashion characteristic of Konrad Adenauer's chancellorship (and remains so of the Adenauer faction in the CDU) the result of the combination is a disposition to look upon any alteration of U.S. support to West Germany—including any suggestions that U.S. troops in Germany might be reduced— as implying a relaxation of the barriers to recognition of East Germany. The same attitude inspires suspicion of any easing of U.S.-Soviet relations, and produced, for example, strong criticism of the treaty banning nuclear tests in the atmosphere. The view reflects the original terms on which the Federal Republic lined up with the West, ignoring or denying that changes of substance have occurred since to alter these terms.

The third pattern of West German thinking about East Germany is different from the first two. It reflects a sense of obligation to do all that is possible and prudent to improve the lot of the people of East Germany. The conflict that may arise between this motive and the legalistic one was evident in the differences of view that emerged between Bonn and Berlin over the Christmas passes. When the possibility of repeating the pass arrangements for Easter was raised, these differences were sufficient to block the proposal. The sense of obligaton to assist the people of East Germany is, of course, by no means always in conflict with the legalistic pattern. Often in the past the decision not to co-operate with Ulbricht could be justified by the West German government on the ground that to help Ulbricht was really against the long-term interests of the people of East Germany.

It is of interest to imagine how these three patterns might be applied if Ulbricht's regime were replaced by a less odious one. Suppose the successor regime successfully survives the transition period without spoiling its new image and immediately begins instituting reforms similar to the nationalist revisions in economic and related policy the East European governments have undertaken. These reforms are successful in making life easier for the East German population, at first by removing some of the more onerous restrictions and, in time, by raising living standards. Simultaneously, the new East German government is relaxing the state's hold on cultural activities and education, so as to encourage the intelligentsia and the students. Finally, the regime begins to give evidence of independence from the Soviet Union on issues of importance to the welfare of the East Germans.

None of this would endear the Communist regime to non-Communist German population that desires above all to be rejoined to the main body of Germany. None of it would change the mind of West Germany about non-recognition of the legitimacy of the East German government. The legalistic pattern of thinking about inter-German relations would, therefore, not be affected.

The West Germans might, however, become convinced that the East German government had gained a significant degree of autonomy from Soviet control and was therefore free to make its own decisions, within broad limits, on issues of importance to the East German people. In that case the West German government might be expected to become convinced of its growing competence to handle inter-German problems without calling upon the United States for support. Further, if Bonn believed that by co-operating the East German government might be encouraged to continue improving the lot of its people, particularly if it also came to believe that its co-operation would tend to increase the autonomy of the East German regime, the West German sense of responsibility would call for more varied, frequent, and friendly relations to this end. Looking rather far ahead, perhaps, one can imagine a time when all inter-German problems would become "German" problems, to be solved by "us Germans."

This development would no doubt be vigorously opposed within West Germany. Whatever the legalistic reservations, however, to many West Germans the policy of improving the lot of the East German people and loosening the Soviet grip would be irresistible, even though reunification remained remote. Indeed, it might well be that support for the policy would become so strong that a West German government that chose to approach its relations with the East in a legalistic and unco-operative spirit would risk giving its oppostition a winning political issue.

It is also likely that the development would be viewed with suspicion from abroad. Despite its supposedly temporary and intolerable character, the division of Germany is nevertheless a status quo with which a variety of diverse interests have learned to coexist. Thus if the merest suggestion that the division might become permanent is anathema to the West Germans, to many outside Germany the prospect of a unified Germany is hardly more palatable. Further, if there is West German concern that the objective of reunification might be betrayed, or at least neglected, in relations between, say, the United States and the Soviet Union, there is no less concern outside of Germany lest the Germans be tempted to make a deal with communism that would be detrimental to the interests of the West as the price of reunion. Nevertheless, if West Germany's partners in NATO and EEC should take a legalistic position opposing a popular move to aid the East German people, or should support an unpopular Bonn policy in this respect, they would risk making continued membership in these international organizations an issue of West German politics.

Ought the prospect of eased relations between West and East Germany by regarded with alarm by the West? Admittedly, the change could be painful, with many occasions arising for misunderstanding between allies. It would not be surprising to see a revival of the latent suspicion of Germany in the British press and in the French parliament. It is perhaps also possible to imagine an overly favorable popular reaction in the U.S., for example, if the West Germans should request the withdrawal of some United States forces in order to support East German efforts to effect the removal of some of the Soviet divisions. Such developments need not gravely affect the unity of the West, however, if their possibility is foreseen and timely steps are taken to minimize them.

This discussion should not be interpreted as a proposal that the United States, or any other power, undertake to push the West Germans into something for which they are not ready or which they regard as contrary to their interest. The problem is theirs, in the first instance, and the choice of tactics in meeting the problem ought to be theirs as well.

In fact, of course, some of the elements of the challenge from East Germany are already in evidence, and so are some elements of the West German response. The lines of engagement within the Federal Republic are already forming. To those who engineered the old policy of non-recognition, and who have upheld it for so many years, every new approach from or to East Germany smacks of concessions and forebodes surrender of the citadel. But the change of relations within and between East and West are facts. It may be called détente and its reversal may be predicted, but so long as the Soviet Union chooses to go along with the change, adding to it direct communications and improved relations with the United States, the atmosphere will continue to clear, and the intransigent positions on both sides in Germany will continue to become decreasingly tenable.

Some Germans and some Americans would have the United States government say to the Kremlin: "You can have better relations in Central Europe only as part of a settlement that includes the unification of Germany with free elections. Otherwise it is Cold War all the way." But it is open to serious question whether the United States government could say this, at least for long, without risking the disintegration of NATO and eventually an adverse popular reaction in the United States. NATO is a defensive coalition; it cannot be expected to support a policy its members, by and large, would consider aggressive. Moreover, even to appear to insist that the world stand at the brink of nuclear war for the sake of an outmoded concept of the way to achieve German reunification could divide the American people.

The frustration of the Old Liners is understandable. They see only what has been happening in Eastern Europe and this they interpret as in indication of growing Communist weakness. Such an indication, of course, is just what they have been waiting for. The West, if somewhat disordered, at least is strong. Look at the five-to-one superiority of the United States over the Soviet Union in ICBM's. The time has come, they feel, to apply the pressure. And if the West lacks the character and fortitude to apply the pressure, then let it at least hold firm.

Against this view, those who try to see developments in a more ample context are forced to point to some difficulties. To be sure, the West is strong. Western Europe is politically stable and self-confident; the NATO members there are prosperous and co-operating in their economic policy; and their heavy investments have paid off, if belatedly, in substantially increased and improved military forces. But if there is, in terms of ready forces, something like a stalemate in Central Europe, and a NATO lead in tactical nuclear weapons to offset the superior mobilization capacity of the Soviet Union, there is on the Soviet side a substantial and uncountered superiority in strategic nuclear power available for use against Western Europe. For this reason as well as the existence of its own ICBM's, despite the great superiority of the United States in striking power over the Arctic, it is unlikely the Soviet Union regards its position as one of weakness. In any case, the position is not one the United States or NATO is tempted to challenge.

It is, indeed, wise to be prepared for setbacks, for moments when future crises in East-West relations register on the tensions gauge in Central Europe. It would be unreasonable to expect the course of altered relations to go forward smoothly. Nevertheless, inter-German relations are unlikely to remain static. The West Germans can no more insist that East Germany is a Soviet stooge and a menace if it ceases to be than the United States can be expected deliberately to perpetuate the Cold War for the sake of the German status quo. In the transition, two perils must be faced. The first is the needless exacerbation of differences within the West; the second is the alienation and eventual defection of West Germany from the West. The key to avoiding both would seem to be a patient and confident understanding among her major NATO partners that permits and encourages the Federal Republic to work out her own new relations with East Germany.

At the same time, the other Western countries are likely to accept any solution of the German question that West Germany itself finds acceptable, so long as the Federal Republic inspires confidence among its partners in the Alliance. Moreover, for the sake of the West's peace of mind, it is desirable, in any case, that West Germany continue to move toward more complete membership in a larger community. Germany is not ready to be cast loose to make her own way in the world, nor is divided Europe ready to make its peace with a Germany that is free and uncontained. It thus seems essential that some European community emerge that is capable of absorbing her. To this end, it is important that NATO be preserved and kept vigorous unless it can be replaced by some better arrangement based upon a more perfectly unified Europe. If NATO is to be kept vigorous in an atmosphere of changed East-West relations, however, sources of strength must be found that do not require that Europe stand on the brink of nuclear war. One of the most important of these sources of strength would be the understanding that the West Germans may work out for themselves the interim relationship with their separated fellow countrymen in East Germany. But other potential sources of strength and stability likewise call for review—notably Western Europe's defenses.

III

Announcing new estimates of Soviet military strength last year, Secretary of Defense Robert L. McNamara pointed to the curious circumstances that by the old estimates the Soviet Union had been supposed, with approximately twice as many men in its ground forces as the United States, to be capable of maintaining ten times the divisions (that is, roughly two million versus one million men and 160 versus 16 divisions). He stated that it had been inferred from this anomaly and from other evidence that a U.S. division must be counted as equivalent to more than one Soviet division. He also said that the estimate of Soviet ready divisions, which had stood at 160 to 175 for over a decade, must be revised sharply downwards, to "less than half." He summarized his new comparison of East-West strength in "battlefield forces" by saying:

. . . the Warsaw Pact [armed forces] total including the Soviets is only about 4.5 million. Against that, it is today the members of NATO whose active armed forces number over five million. The ground forces of NATO nations total 3.2 million, of which 2.2 million men are in Europe, as against the Soviet ground combat forces total of about 2 million men, and a Warsaw Pact total of about 3 million. Both the Soviet Union and the U.S. forces of course include units stationed in the Far East. *In Central Europe, NATO has more men, and more combat troops, on the ground than does the Bloc. It has more men on the ground in West Germany than the Bloc does in East Germany. It has more and better tactical aircraft, and these planes can carry twice the payload twice as far as the Soviet counterparts.*[7]

The Secretary's purpose was to encourage the European members of NATO to make better provision for conventional (i.e., non-nuclear) defense, by indicating to them that the task was by no means beyond their reach. What got across, however, was the impression that the threat of attack by an overwhelmingly superior conventional force from the East was no more.

It is also of interest that Soviet forces in East Germany and Poland appear to have remained roughly the same, at about 300,000, since before the Korean War. To be sure, East German armed forces of around 110,000 were built up during this period. At the same time, however, U.S. forces in Europe were being increased from about 80,000, around 1950, to more than 300,000 today, and West German armed forces of nearly 400,000 men were created.

If there is still, or for that matter ever was, an "aggressive" threat from East to West in Central Europe, with conventional forces, it must be embodied in the impressive Soviet mobilization potential. Mr. McNamara, indeed, took note that, as reported by Chairman Khrushchev in January, 1960, the mobilization of Soviet armed forces had reached a peak of five and three-quarter million in 1955—explained by Khrushchev "as a result of the formation of the aggressive NATO bloc in the West and the atom bomb blackmail at the time when we had none. . . ." From that time onwards, however, according to the same statement, the Soviet forces total had fallen, to about 3.5 million at the time Khrushchev spoke.[8]

---

[7] Remarks before the Economic Club of New York, November 18, 1963. Emphasis added.

[8] The corresponding figure for the fall of 1963, according to the Institute for Strategic Studies, was 3.3 million. In the speech referred to, Khrushchev announced his intention of making further reductions, to under 2.5 million. These were not carried through, owing, it was later stated, to the increases in United States armed forces that occurred in 1961 and 1962.

It is worthy of emphasis that this decline in the standing conventional forces threat to Western Europe, which was to be described by official spokesmen as "overwhelming" for another seven years, began just as the first West Germans were finally entering upon their military training. The conclusion suggested is that not since 1956 have the Soviets tried to maintain, in regular forces available for conventional war, the numerically superior *capability* that bespeaks aggressive *intentions*.

From this and other indications it appears to be possible, without imprudence, to establish the pattern of evolving Soviet armed strength from before the Korean War. The pattern gives a definite impression of Soviet defense priorities, and no feature of it clearly signals an intention of launching aggressive attacks anywhere.

The Soviet armed "threat" to Western Europe is now, and has been since nuclear military power became a two-sided affair, primarily the threat of an all-out effort, beginning with a bomber and missile nuclear attack and followed (if that is conceivable) by a "broken-back" invasion phase, which would likewise involve the employment of nuclear weapons. Perhaps until the late fifties it was still possible to conceive that a massive conventional attack through Germany was a plausible alternative. Until German rearmament was well under way it was a fact that the NATO forces were ill-prepared to stop such an attack without resort to nuclear weapons, and it was barely conceivable the Soviets might doubt the West's willingness to make the decision to start a nuclear war. It was to preclude Soviet miscalculation of this kind that the United States government then, as now, laid such stress upon its superior capability of strategic attack upon the armed forces of the Soviet Union.

The Soviet Union, of course, still possesses the capacity to launch a substantial non-nuclear attack upon Western Europe. The forces for such an attack, however, are in

Western Russia, not in Eastern Europe, and they could not be brought forward without giving NATO days, and perhaps weeks, of warning. Further, it appears they may have become as dependent upon battlefield nuclear weapons as it was feared a few years ago the NATO forces were becoming (though the Russians are not bemused by the smallest nuclear warheads, such as the Davey Crockett). Finally, with or without using nuclear weapons, the forces are hardly of sufficient strength to inspire the Russian military staffs with confidence in their success unless they are reinforced by a general mobilization—which would give NATO additional warning.

Are such forces evidence of intention to commit military aggression? It seems unlikely. Against an enemy devoid of nuclear power the Soviet missile threat would be admirably suited to blackmail and intimidation, which is the reason both that a U.S. commitment to the defense of Western Europe is vital to the area's continued progress and confidence and that Britain and France have been so eager to possess independent "deterrents." Against a power possessing nuclear forces of its own, however—assuming that these deterrent forces are not highly vulnerable to destruction in a surprise nuclear attack—for the Soviets to employ their forces for aggressive purposes would be an act of self-destruction.

This is to reduce the problem of NATO strength to its barest essentials. Moreover, to consider that this is all there is to it would be as misguided as the original simplification that the peril against which the West must be girded was the imminent threat of surprise attack by overwhelming masses of Communist manpower armed only with non-nuclear weapons. Forces that exist have a variety of capabilities, including some that were possibly not even thought of when they were being planned. Further, national motives, like personal ones, are never simple. Thus it is evident that the Soviet Union and its allies do possess the capacity for limited conventional and nuclear attacks against the NATO forces, both in the center and at the wings. Because they do have this capacity, even though it may be doubted that a significant reason for creating the forces was to provide it, NATO must prepare itself to meet or deter the capacity.

The foregoing remarks are in no sense intended to suggest that military strength in the Western Europe was not needed to deal with the threat from the East, nor that NATO was an inappropriate instrumentality through which to provide it. On the contrary, granted the Soviet respect for military power, not to say the Communist disposition to justify the use of military power for any legitimate, i.e., Communist, purpose, strengthening Western Europe's defense was indispensable. In addition, if the West Germans were to share the burden, and if Western Europe were to be protected from Soviet, nuclear blackmail without extensive proliferation of the possession of nuclear weapons, the entanglement of the United States in this enterprise, both as an occupier of Germany and as the only nuclear power, was inescapable. It does not appear, however, that the United States' contribution to NATO forces in Europe, which was set at six divisions in 1951, need have been a perpetual and even an irreducible commitment. What was also not inescapable, moreover, was the perpetuation for a decade and a half of the warlike and unstable posture NATO has given its forces on the plea that they must be at all times prepared for a massive surprise attack from the East.

One example of this posture is the expansion of its tactical air force, to which NATO devoted some of its most strenuous and effective efforts during its first decade.[9] The end product of these efforts is a powerful force of

---

[9] I am indebted to Carl H. Amme, Jr., of the Stanford Research Institute for calling this aspect of the instability in Europe to my attention.

some thousands of high-performance fighter bombers, potentially if not currently armed with nuclear bombs, crowding a comparatively small number of airfields. These planes were highly vulnerable to enemy surprise attack even before the Russians began to deploy missiles. In the standard corpus of the new strategy the confrontation of nuclear air forces, each highly vulnerable to surprise attack, each highly effective in launching surprise attack, is the epitome of military instability.

Or consider the introduction into NATO forces of tactical nuclear weapons and the growing dependence of these forces on these weapons. Until the trend was reversed by the Kennedy Administration, the tendency had been not only to increase the number and variety of battlefield nuclear delivery systems, and the warheads to go with them, but also to deploy these weapons farther and farther toward the front, until the Davey Crockett nuclear bazooka was about to fall into the hands of front-line battalion commanders. A defense that delegates the *power* of decision for nuclear war that far down the line (regardless of where the *authority* to make the decision is held) cannot be considered serious in its intention to embrace nuclear war only as the final resort. Fortunately, this error was corrected and the Davey Crocketts were withdrawn to the rear where there would be some chance of exercising responsible control over the decision to initiate their employment.

The contribution of NATO forces to military instability in Europe is not, however, confined to a list of such specific items. It stems from broader origins than that, notably the conception of the mission, which keeps the forces in a state of semialert, from the way the commitment to nuclear defense has evolved, and most basic of all, from the insistence upon the tactics of a mobile or fluid defense. These are all complex issues that will be examined in detail in the remainder of this discussion.

The European NATO governments, supported by most European strategists, amateur and professional, have resisted the urgings of the United States government that they strengthen NATO's conventional defenses. At the same time they have been critical of the preference of the United States for reducing reliance upon nuclear weapons for front-line defense. At least until the McNamara speech quoted earlier, however, their reason for thus diverging from United States policy was not that the conventional threat had been exaggerated. Rather, it was that the NATO requirement is for deterrence, not defense. They were unwilling to assume the heavier burdens of an increased conventional defense they deemed unnecessary so long as the tactical nuclear threat was available as a substitute, and to justify this opposition they professed to fear that if the emphasis upon non-nuclear defense was increased, the Russians might actually be encouraged to attack.

There is still this fear that the United States will insist upon "overcontrolling" the tactical nuclear weapons. It is one of two major sources of the growing European discontent at their dependence upon U.S. nuclear power. The other relates to the possession and control of strategic nuclear power. The reason for the latter concern is, of course, the vulnerability of Western Europe to the great nuclear power—borne by fighter bombers, medium bombers, and missiles of various ranges—the Soviet Union can bring to bear against it. The NATO military staffs conceive the problem as one of "targeting." Can the NATO forces effectively, and convincingly, target Soviet airfields and medium and intermediate range missiles?

The answer, at the moment, is that NATO cannot, at least not without substantial help from the United States' Strategic Air Command. Partly because of this dependence, when responsible United States authorities talk about the conventional "pause"—the period after a Soviet conventional attack starts and before it becomes evident that the attack justifies a nuclear response—the European NATO reaction is unfavorable. There is fear that the talk may convince the Soviet Union it could seize some part of the NATO territory, say, Hamburg, while the United States is making up its mind to halt the enemy advance by resorting to nuclear weapons, and that the prize might be held long enough to bargain for its release against some desired Communist objective. Reinforcing nervousness about the desire of the United States to withdraw the tactical nuclear weapons from the forward elements on the central front, this worry feeds the demand for a European voice in the control of nuclear weapons.

Presumably it is believed that the Russians are less likely to suspect the European powers of reluctance to employ these nuclear weapons in defense of their own territory than they are of being tempted by U.S. reluctance to hazard the safety of American cities in nuclear war. The proposal for a multilateral force (MLF) of shipborne Polaris missiles, purchased from the United States, is the response of the government of the United States to this European concern. The MLF would be under NATO control and the ships would be manned by integrated crews from several countries, so that no one country could paralyze the force by withdrawing its contribution or diverting its share of the force to national purposes.

It has been suggested by some students of the problem of nuclear control that the issue is not properly one of the ultimate decision—the finger on the trigger or the safety catch—but rather one of planning. If the countries principally concerned were permitted adequate participation in the planning of NATO programs and operations, the argument runs, they would learn enough about the uses and limits of nuclear weapons to satisfy themselves that the issues were being responsibly handled; and they would see the virtue of leaving the ultimate decision to resort to nuclear weapons to an unambiguous, i.e., single, authority.

Others would argue, however, that broad participation in nuclear planning is already being permitted, with no perceptible effect upon the conflict over nuclear control.

There is no obvious solution to the dilemma, but there is no doubt of the question that emerges: Is the U.S. prepared to transfer the responsibility for the ultimate decision to NATO as a body or, alternatively, to some smaller grouping of European powers? Some of the official promoters of the multilateral force have more than hinted that the latter is the case. They suggest that ownership and control of the MLF, including its nuclear warheads, will be vested in a separate international organization, though within NATO, of the members participating in the MLF. They suggest further that once such an organization has been set up and is functioning properly, the U.S. will abandon its "veto," i.e., its ultimate control, leaving the decision to employ the force to some delegated or majority-decision processes as yet undetermined.

Those American officials who favor relinquishment of the U.S. veto on the use of the MLF presumably view it as encouraging the Europeans to move toward greater unity. They also hope that it will encourage the British and eventually the French to give up the burdensome effort to maintain an independent national nuclear deterrent force, and that it will forestall the emergence of similar ambitions in the Federal Republic. It should be added that without the devolution of nuclear control the MLF proposal is bound to impress many Europeans (and perhaps many Americans as well) as essentially phony—a device for flimflamming the Germans into believing they have acquired status as a nuclear power while continuing to deny them that status in fact.

The German government, however, appears to take a rather different view of the matter, regarding the MLF as a useful device for tying the United States that much more closely to the nuclear defense of Western Europe. This view of course rests on the assumption that the United States, along with other participants, would be unable to withdraw its participation (and the missiles and warheads it supplied) from the MLF without unanimous agreement.

The German government may also regard the MLF as a way of successfully resisting French pressures to form a Franco-German (or continental) nuclear entente that would be led as well as supplied with nuclear weapons by France and designed to reduce U.S. influence: Bonn does want to be forced to make an explicit choice between Washington and Paris. It is also possible, of course, that the West German government believes the MLF will evolve toward autonomy from the United States and regards this as a desirable step toward the unification of Europe, which it strongly supports. Thus far the only signs of this expectation have been statements from some West Germans, notably the Minister of Defense, looking to eventual agreed revisions to the initial unanimous control formula for the MLF that would subsitute a majority voice, possibly weighted to reflect relative shares in the financial support of the force. The immediate occasion for these statements, however, is apparently the desire of the West German government, with its acute interest in the integrity of the nuclear deterrent threat, to eliminate the possibility of an Italian or British veto, which it sees as diluting that threat and consequently its deterrent effect.[10]

There is no need, for purposes of this discussion, to explore further the interesting problems of the MLF, which have been mentioned only as illustrating the United States' response to the European concern over the integrity of the nuclear deterrent. As a much less vulnerable substitute for part of the NATO fighter-bomber force, if it indeed turns out to be that, the MLF could contribute substan-

---

[10] For an able analytical examination, see Robert E. Osgood, *The Case for the MLF: A Critical Evaluation* (The Washington Center of Foreign Policy Research, 1964).

tially to stability. By not having to be trigger happy, it is better suited to the long-term, "peacetime" defense establishment toward which the NATO defense needs to move. In so far as it served its purpose of reducing NATO's dependence on the nuclear power of the United States, the MLF would not only weaken the ties of this country to Western Europe, it would also reduce the *military* need for continued United States involvement in NATO Europe's defense.

Returning to the problem of conventional forces and non-nuclear defense, it is important to note that there is general agreement that NATO should not have to resort immediately to nuclear weapons in every possible military contingency. Even the West Germans, who are strongest in insistence on the commitment to tactical nuclear weapons for the sake of deterrence, readily agree it is conceivable that small-scale probes, border incidents, or other explosive situations might arise to which it would be absurd to respond by early use of nuclear weapons. The difficulty is, as pointed out earlier, that they also regard the nuclear commitment as the cornerstone of NATO's deterrent posture. This being the case, the West Germans are readier to chance precipitation of an inadvertent nuclear war by NATO miscalculation of Communist intent than they are to risk the possibility of the Soviet miscalculation they perceive if the deterrent effect of the commitment to early use of nuclear weapons is in any way diminished.

The preference for reliance upon nuclear weapons is abetted by the deployment and tactics of the NATO defenses. To be sure, some of the units have been assigned a blocking role—that is, they are to move forward upon alert and take up defensive positions; nevertheless, the basic tactical concept is that of a fluid defense. The NATO forces are designed for mobility, and there are designated but no prepared defensive positions. With only a thin screen of armored cavalry in front of them, it may even be questioned whether, in event of the surprise attack they are intended to halt, the blocking units would even reach their assigned positions. In any case, the mounting of a successful, fluid defense is critically dependent upon time being available to determine which are the attacker's major thrusts. Time is also required to organize and launch the counterattacks by armored and mechanized forces from the rear that are the *pièce de résistance* of such a defense, and to which other divisions are currently assigned. For these reasons a mobile defense requires space, and space is the scarcest military resource on the central front.[11]

The NATO command may have been compelled to adopt the fluid defense tactics by the realization that it could not expect the European NATO governments to maintain standing forces adequate to provide coverage for the central front, although there is also ground for suspicion that the preferred tactics reflect a military bias favoring a fluid defense. The conventional forces' goals, set at Lisbon in February, 1952, did endeavor to provide coverage of the front, but the Lisbon concept required mobilization to fill the ranks to the necessary strength. Convinced that war in the nuclear age would be "short," and anticipating a virtual United States monopoly of "tactical" nuclear weapons, the military staffs gave up reliance on this mobilization with no great resistance when it became apparent the schedules were not, in any case, going to be met by the member governments.

Abandonment of the requirement that the front be covered, however, involved a penalty. The consequence of

---

[11] NATO plans also call for the mobilization of additional units from the reserves in event of attack. In time these should serve to stiffen the defense. The above discussion is concerned, however, with what happens immediately following the attack and while the reserves (which are not militia ready for immediate action on their home grounds) are being mustered and moved around.

dependence upon a fluid defense with mobile forces has been to present the military authorities and governments with the uncomfortable alternatives, in the event of a non-nuclear engagement, either of yielding territory or of resorting almost immediately to nuclear weapons.

Abandonment of the goal of providing forward coverage for the NATO central front may also have had another considerable disadvantage. This was to suggest to the prospective enemy a NATO proclivity to pre-empt—that is, to attack first and force *him* to trade space for time. The fact that the strongest NATO force on the central front, the Seventh United States Army, is located where it is (mostly from Frankfurt eastward into Bavaria)—although the location came about for essentially non-military reasons—may also serve to convince any Russian general who thinks about it that the mission of the force *must* be to seize Prague, or at least Leipzig, possibly the day before an attack from the East is expected.

In brief, even in their conventional embodiment, because of their character and deployment, NATO forces on the critical central front contribute excessively to the instability of the confrontation. In fact, it requires no great vicarious effort on our part to realize how, from the Russian point of view, it must appear (as until quite recently it has appeared to the United States the other way around) that their adversary is poised for offensive action the moment their guard is lowered.

It is indeed true that the confrontation has survived a remarkable number of serious crises, three of which—the Hungarian Rebellion (1956), the Berlin crisis of 1958–61, and the Cuban showdown of 1962—have occurred since the commitment was made to nuclear weapons in lieu of conventional forces adequate to cover the front. Nevertheless, the instability of the confrontation is recognized, as evidenced by the welling sense of panic in Western Europe that accompanies every such crisis of the Cold War. In the past, though not recently, the United States government has had more than one occasion to complain that this reaction imposed hampering restraints upon its freedom of action, sometimes in crises remote from Central Europe. The difficulty is that the same nuclear stalemate the Europeans find so comforting in non-crisis times (i.e., when the tempo of the Cold War is "normal") becomes transformed into a source of fear, and consequently of weakness, when cold-war tempers rise.

What is to be done about it? There is no question that the forces currently available to NATO are insufficient to alleviate the dangers of nuclear overreliance and miscalculation. But this matter of numbers is not the only inadequacy nor would raising the ready forces to thirty divisions, as the United States has been trying to do for some years, remedy the situation.

Thirty divisions would, in fact, be only a little less inadequate to the requirement than the current twenty-five. Indeed, the addition might augment the offensive image of the NATO forces rather more than it would raise their effectiveness on the defensive. Opinions about this may differ, but studies that preceded setting the Lisbon goals in 1952 indicated a minimum requirement for about fifty divisions to provide central-front, forward coverage against a major conventional attack. Nor did this number include the forces required to launch counterattacks against enemy penetrations; it was merely the force designed to slow the attackers' advance. Even so, it appears to have been the opinion of the military that the main line of the NATO defense would be on the Rhine.

The reason for this was not only their exaggerated respect for the power of a Soviet offensive. It was also a consequence of their addiction to a fluid defense. Hence the feeling, seldom admitted once the decision was made to arm the Germans, that it would be impossible to hold a determined attack east of the Rhine, and the unavowed resolve to use the Rhine as a substitute for prepared defenses.

While there was considerable criticism of this defense concept in the Federal Republic, because it recalled past experience with "scorched earth" and "liberation," the concept prevailed.[12] The reason, it appears, is that the West Germans, like other West Europeans, soon learned to rely upon predominant U.S. nuclear power—in strategic and, later, in tactical nuclear weapons—to overawe the enemy. It is believed, hopefully, that the Russians would not risk attack while the irreducible uncertainty involved in doing so includes the possiblility of a holocaust in which their homeland would be consumed.

This is of course "massive retaliation" all over again, the difference being that the mutuality of the strategic threat does not arouse fears of a stalemate under which the Communists might feel justified in risking limited aggressive action, if the presence of tactical nuclear weapons, and an early and ineluctable commitment to their use, successfully links the local situation to the intercontinental one.

Reliance on the "rational tactic of uncertainty" is, however, hardly a happy choice for the United States.[13] It may even be that if the European members of NATO—and specifically the Federal Republic of Germany—were in a position of responsibility, rather than privileged to transfer

---

[12] Opposition to the NATO concept within the Blank Office, predecessor to the Defense Ministry of the Federal Republic, was voiced by Colonel Bogislav von Bonin, chief of the planning section, who favored a forward static defense. When he carried his objections to the public, Colonel von Bonin was dismissed. For brief accounts of the incident see Henry A. Kissinger, *Nuclear Weapons and Foreign Policy* (New York: Harper, 1957), pp. 288–91 and Alastair Buchan and Philip Windsor, *Arms and Stability in Europe* (London: Chatto & Windus, 1963), pp. 39–40.

[13] The phrase is from Alastair Buchan and Philip Windsor, *Arms and Stability in Europe,* p. 152.

the problem of nuclear deterrence to the United States, they too would see its shortcomings.

The tactical "minimum deterrent," even when hinged to United States nuclear strategic superiority of some substance, hardly fills the requirement. The reason is not only that, because of it, some miscalculated or precipitate action may call upon the United States to sacrifice itself, and a fair fraction of humanity, as an alternative to seeing some local crisis through; it is also because, over a wide range of possible events, the tactical nuclear deterrent is both excessively accident prone and insufficiently credible.

There are, moreover, many crisis situations in which the ability and willingness to *do* something to prove determination to resist is vastly more significant than suicidal talk. This should have been proved to the satisfaction of the West Europeans not only by the Cuban crisis of 1962 (the lesson of which they are disposed to depreciate because of the "overwhelming" United States conventional advantage at the crisis scene) but also by the Berlin crisis of 1961 that occasioned the sending of some 70,000 additional American soldiers to Europe.

What NATO requires—generally, but specifically on the critical central front—is a more credible *defense* to lend credibility to its *deterrent*. Further, taking into account not only the revised estimates of Soviet capabilities and intentions and the mounting importance of nuclear weapons but also the changes in the political environment, it is desirable that this defense be one that can be successfully maintained over the long pull, that it not impress the opponents to the East as potentially threatening and provocative, and that it not be such as to arouse panic in Western Europe at moments when the need for it is most acute.

To minimize the impact of nuclear blackmail from the East, that defense must obviously be "nuclear." But if the defense is to be convincing it must also be something else (something less or more, depending upon the point of view) than reliance upon tactical nuclear weapons and their explicit threat of escalation to holocaust—for the same reason that we do not arm museum guards with hand grenades. It therefore demands a solution to that most vexing of the problems of contemporary local defense: the combination of nuclear and non-nuclear weapons and forces. Further, if it is to be suitable for confined areas such as West Germany, the defense cannot be, in its non-nuclear embodiment, fluid.

There are of course great difficulties in changing the basic planning concepts of a structure as complex and as fraught with political compromise as NATO. Moreover, the outsider naturally hesitates before making suggestions in so specialist a field. Nevertheless, NATO is being subjected to severe re-examination as this is written. Already a few American writers are calling for its abandonment, arguing that the Alliance is no longer needed for the defense of Europe and that to preserve it as a device for maintaining United States influence in Western Europe will produce increasing friction in the West while obstructing progress toward better relations between the United States and the Soviet Union.[14] As I do not share either of these views, I shall overcome my scruples and suggest a way of possible escape from these NATO shortcomings.

This suggestion is that the kind of defense NATO requires can best be achieved by substituting a radically different tactical concept for the present one, with its almost total dependence upon standing forces and explicit early reliance on tactical nuclear weapons. The alternative concept calls for a forward prepared defense, partially manned with regular troops but relying upon the mobilization base to fill out the front coverage when crises loom. This defense would deter the prospective attacker, in the first instance, by confronting him with an extremely tough

---

[14] See particularly Ronald Steel, *The End of Alliance: America and the Future of Europe* (New York: Viking, 1964).

conventional barrier, the tactical nuclear option being held in reserve.[15]

It would not, of course, be possible to make so drastic a shift quickly. Rather, what ought to be envisioned is the establishment of new goals for NATO planning and the institution of orderly programs aimed at achieving them in due course. The transition period will be less than an ideal, but at least the direction will be sound (and, after all, NATO has been in a stultified transition for some years).

This planning objective, then, would be a defense-in-depth barrier consisting of three major components. First, there would be forward fixed positions, prepared defenses, permanently manned by a non-mobile part of the standing force. Ideally, perhaps, these elements might occupy underground forts arranged in several parallel lines and creating a barrier zone perhaps forty miles deep. During the transition they would necessarily be given less protection; moreover, experience and the indicated staff studies might lead to the conclusion that there are better ways to man the barrier than with fixed underground positions. Whatever their form, the role of these positions would be either to limit the attacker's choice among points for assault and exposing the flanks of his spearheads or to force him to assault them directly. If the latter were his choice, depending upon how heavily protected the defensive positions were, it would be more and more difficult, and it ought ultimately to be virtually impossible, for him to launch a surprise attack, because of the advanced preparations that would be necessary. The permanent forward positions would have an additional role no less important than the first, which is to serve as centers of communica-

---

[15] Similar concepts were proposed in Germany at the time when the form that German rearmament should take was being debated, notably by the military commentator Adelbert Weinstein, in his little book *Nieman Kann den Krieg Gewinnen* (Bonn: Schimmelbusch, 1955). His position resembled that of Colonel von Bonin referred to in note 12.

tion and fire support for the second elements of the forward defense.[16]

This second element of the forward defense would likewise be composed of prepared positions, though the preparations could be much less elaborate. These positions would not be permanently occupied. Instead, they would be manned by local militia and other reserve units, which would assemble for practice periodically and would be subject to immediate call whenever the onset of a crisis indicated a need to man the frontiers.[17] They would be located in the villages, towns, and cities of the battle zone, or in wooded and hilly areas if that should be indicated by the terrain.

The third major element of the defense would be the maneuver force, as at present. This would consist of armored, mechanized, and possibly airborne units, available to plug gaps torn in the forward defense zone by the attack and to mount concentrated counterattacks against major penetrations.

The advantages of this arrangement will be clear from what has gone before in the discussion. Several points, however, are worthy of special emphasis. One is that only with the addition of prepared defenses is the deployment of the defenses of West Germany forward toward the frontiers possible without grossly increasing the pressure to resort to battlefield nuclear weapons. The time an attacker would need to breach the forward defenses would of course also be available to the maneuver elements of the defense to the rear, enormously increasing their effectiveness. With such a defense in depth it would be a mas-

---

[16] Even if the actual defense positions were not underground or concrete forts the command, communications, and fire control centers would need to be.

[17] The case for militia, based upon Swiss experience, has been made in persuasive detail by Frederick Martin Stern in his book *The Citizen Army, Key to Defense in the Atomic Age* (New York: St. Martin's Press, 1957).

sive conventional attack indeed that could force the defenders to make an early choice to resort to tactical nuclear weapons. Further, as such a mass attack would require massive preparations, it would assure that the defense would be at maximum strength before the attack hit it. Another point is that the permanently occupied forward positions commanded by general officers would make it possible to retain the short-range tactical nuclear delivery weapons in protected locations in the forward area without committing them to use at the option of a battalion commander. A third point is that these same positions would enable the defense to mount a fairly elaborate anti-aircraft missile defense, placing an AA umbrella over the battlefield. A final point, not previously mentioned, is the political advantage of a defense that can be promptly and visibly strengthened to give evidence of determination in crises.

Despite the obvious and no doubt unhappy parallel to the ill-fated Maginot line, this concept is capable of considerable flexibility. Not only is the permanent occupancy of the barrier zone given to varied interpretation (an alternative proposal to that made here, which others have favored, calls for highly mobile but specialized forces to occupy the barrier zone), but also its depth, its strength in permanent units, the density of coverage in time of alert, and the effort on prepared positions may all be varied.

Without detailed studies based chiefly upon sensitive information, it is impossible to determine what the troop requirements of such a defense would be and what it would cost. A very rough estimate indicates that the Federal Republic could obtain a defense that is a substantial improvement on all counts over the current defense with fewer permanent troops than NATO now maintains on the central front, though only if the permanent force were supplemented with a substantial body of militia and reserves. The cost for real estate and construction would be high. So, however, are permanent divisions, and no rough estimate will indicate which of the two concepts is the more costly in the long run.

It is probably not to be expected that the proposed concept would be favorably received by the NATO military staffs. Most military professionals (East as well as West) are still under the spell of World War II. Moreover, they are finding it hard enough to accommodate their thinking to the introduction of nuclear weapons, without the added insult of being asked to make what they must regard as the retrogressive step to position-defense thinking. Nor is it to be expected that the concept will be popular, at least at first glance, with the people most directly affected, the West Germans. For them, in addition to the certainty of a larger proportional troop contribution, in the form of militia force of perhaps half a million or even more, the problem of acquiring the needed real estate in a crowded country, and the expectation of higher costs, will be added the perhaps crowning objection that the concept would appear to build another and more definitive wall between themselves and the East Germans. Finally, the other European NATO governments might be expected to boggle at such an added "militarization" of the Germans, and this would no doubt be the initial reaction to the East as well.

All these are serious objections, particularly the problems created for the West Germans. Yet none of them appears to be insuperable if it is recognized that a problem exists that demands solution. On the objection to establishing the barrier between West and East Germany, for example, the concept might first be applied to the Czech border. It could then be extended northward only after its advantages had been realized, including the expected long-run effect of stablizing relations with the East.

This assumes, of course, that there is actually a desire to

stabilize relations in Central Europe, a desire it is not clear
now exists. It is for this reason that the proposed change in
NATO's defense concept is put forward in a discussion that
revolves around the change in East-West relations. If the
analysis of the problem is competent, the barrier defense
concept would strengthen NATO militarily in any context.
But a special need for it arises if the assessment is correct that there is a greater danger of war in Central Europe as a result of the combination of acute if suspended
political contests and unstable military relations than from
the adversary's "aggressiveness."

IV

Does anyone, anywhere, still believe that Germany will
be reunited in the end only if the West maintains a position
of strength from which to impose its will upon a Soviet
Union grown too weak to resist or too indifferent to care?
If so, they are surely members of a small minority. To
most of us, the only light at the end of that particular tun-
nel is a fireball.

Does anyone, anywhere, still believe in the *imminent*
threat of surprise attack from the East? Here the negative
is resounding. In fact, it has been some years since even
the NATO military staffs credited this threat.

NATO's sturdiest champions, however, would have us
proceed as though both these formulations are as sound today as when they were first evolved. Otherwise, they say, the
West Germans will consider themselves betrayed and the
armed strength of the Alliance will disappear—both with
catastrophic effects upon the West's unity and security.

But can that unity and security survive upon so fictional
a base? True, many of us would say that democratic
unity always rests upon political myths. But those myths
concern values and relations about which there is *no* ob-

jective truth. Deliberate fictions describing specific issues are another matter altogether. They may not be questioned, hence will not be revealed as fictions, while the conditions they are supposed to reflect are novel and intimidating; but in the long run, when their sandy foundations are revealed, they become provocations disruptive of the unity of a free society.

It is interesting to reflect, in this connection, that five or so years ago some of those who are now most vigorous in their defense of orthodoxy were saying that no one really desired the reunion of Germany, not even the West Germans. It is a tribute to the growing influence of the Federal Republic, and to the constancy of its people to their highest aspiration, that this tune has changed. And well it has, for it too much resembled another, sometimes still heard, according to which "after all, it was the Germans who started World War II and lost it, and therefore must expect to pay for it." Neither cynicism is a possible theme upon which to build the harmony of the West.

The West's most urgent need, then, is for mutual trust and the candor to go with it. But there is a need for realism too. For example, the mind of the West, which runs to historical precedents, must resolutely reject those of Europe's classic irredenta, the Alsace-Lorraines that counsel despair in the nuclear era and turn to other precedents, to Austria or the Saar, that promise the peaceful adjustment of territorial arrangements offensive to the spirit of a people.

In this perspective surely the odds favor the Germans. The military occupation of East Germany is an affront to them, as indeed it is to the West at large. But it is also a damning confession of weakness on the part of German communism and a contradiction of the principle of Marxist-Leninism that every people must make and maintain its own revolution. The principle limits the outsider, even the "socialist homeland," to aid in crises; it does not warrant military occupation of a people "not yet ready for revolution." The longer the occupation of East Germany endures the more obvious it becomes that the East German regime is fraudulent and the more the Soviet Union must depend upon denunciations of Germanism, *per se,* to justify its continued military presence. But what happens to those denunciations as the West Germans enmesh themselves ever more deeply in the West's affairs while sharing the increasingly normal relations with the Communist principalities in Eastern Europe? In time, one would suppose, the Russians must either begin looking for reasons to withdraw their troops from German territory, or else abandon their own claims to respectability in the socialist commonwealth they now seem hopefully to be evolving. When this happens the only question will be whether the East Germans have, in fact, been converted to communism. The delay is tragic, but if the German people remain firm in their hopes, it seems impossible the East German saga can have other than a happy ending for them.

On the military front, meanwhile, surely the fact that the nuclear colossus to the East exists is sufficient reason for the West to be united and strong.

The stability or instability of the relations of adversary nations is admittedly an obscure amalgam of many influences. Thwarted national aspirations or a nagging sense of national insecurity are the psychological forces that probably most commonly underlie the international politics of discontent. Armed, this discontent becomes "aggressiveness" to its putative victims. But not all "aggressors" are Tamerlanes or Hitlers. There are degrees of fear and ambition as of strength, not to say of prudence.

Experience supports the proposition that to oppose armed discontent requires arms. But experience also teaches that the armament required to contain a threatening presence is different from that needed to repel a threatened attack. True, the somber vision of a nuclear Pearl Harbor is acutely distressing, so distressing, indeed, that the soldier is reluctant to agree that potential or "peacetime" military power suffices to deter a nuclear "enemy." One is reminded, however, of 1914, and of the penalty of so emphasizing the decisiveness of mobilizing first that mobilization and war became inevitable. The consequences of that preoccupation with readiness are as well known as they are inadequate to measure the price we shall pay if the error is repeated in our era.

De Gaulle's Designs for
Europe and the West

by
Jean-Baptiste Duroselle *

What are the gradual and profound transformations that the passage of time has brought to the East-West conflict? In what measure can Western unity—if such unity is not really a myth—influence this evolution in a sense favorable to the way of liberty? To what degree does "Western unity" imply American leadership? Must Western Europe increase her autonomy under this leadership, or should she retain her position for the sake of the larger order? Is it necessary to unify Europe before creating an "Atlantic partnership," or would it be better to overlook this first difficult measure and create at once an institutionalized "Atlantic community?" What type of European unity should be suggested on the juridical level (the degree of supranationality) and on the geographical level (the Six only, or the inclusion of England and other partners)? These are the questions facing Europe today, questions which promote divergent views and which are greatly

* *Jean-Baptiste Duroselle:* Professor at the Sorbonne, Director of the Centre d'Étude des Relations Internationales, Paris. Former visiting lecturer at Notre Dame, Harvard, Bologna Centre of the School of Advanced International Studies, The Johns Hopkins University. Has written on religious history, diplomatic history, and international relations. Has taught in the Universities of Saarbrucken and Lille.

changed from the questions posed in the Stalin era, when Europe was weak and "blood-let."

The object of this paper is to try to determine, whenever possible, what could be the responses of General de Gaulle to these questions. Difficulties appear immediately. The problem of the interpretation of Gaullism has become one of the leitmotivs of editors and political scientists. This man generates impassioned reaction and interest the world over. A given issue of the *New York Times* has six articles relating to de Gaulle on page one. In every discussion or colloquy on "Europe and the United States," he, more than any other statesman, especially since the tragic death of President Kennedy, is the subject of conversation. We are bound to admit, then, the existence of a "Gaullist phenomenon" which dominates the beginning of the nineteen-sixties. This phenomenon is that the leader of a secondary power, France, holds in the eyes of the press a role which is out of proportion with the relatively weak potentialities of his country. The problem, or one of the problems at least, is to see whether the position which he occupies in the determination of international relations merits the consideration which he receives in the press.

There are few persons who can approach this problem objectively. On the one hand there are the impassioned Gaullists who see in him the dominating figure of the second half of our century. For these people he is a brilliant prophet of the future, an incomparable strategist whose views are long-range ones and whose calculations are magically accurate, a tactician with amazing facility, logical, coolheaded, and awesome; he is the "man of the twenty-first century." On the other hand, there are the impassioned anti-Gaullists, numerous in all the countries of the West including France, who find in him the same characteristics seen not as virtues but rather as attributes of evil, a diabolical genius which corrodes everything and which prevents the worthy men from coming to the top. Sometimes these critics, like Joseph Alsop, bolster their position by stating that de Gaulle is a mediocre strategist and a detestable tactician. They like to affirm that he is lost in the past, "a man of the nineteenth century."

But there are very few persons who seek to analyze Gaullism objectively. The value of such an analysis is to reduce the amplitudes of the hypotheses, to avoid the multiplication of baseless interpretations, and to evaluate only on the basis of the spoken word and the accomplished act. The spoken word is, of course, difficult to interpret, because the General has deliberately chosen a style that is all his own and which is intentionally ambiguous. We will return to this point later. But actions, as compared to words, present the advantage of being well defined. They permit one to interpret the spoken word and to see more clearly the basic lines of Gaullist diplomacy. In the long run, one might say that these lines are neither as straight as his supporters claim, nor as sinuous as they are said to be by his opponents.

We are going to try to describe these lines as they appear to us, an effort which has at its foundations two successive analyses: one, more substantial, concerns *tactics* and *method* (style), while the other, less certain, has to do with long-range plans or, if one may say, with *diplomatic strategy*.

The Immediate Goals: Gaullist Tactics

From 1958 to 1962, the Algerian problem dominated everything. The war there had to be brought to a close without provoking another generalized revolt of the army. This goal was attained. The repercussions—the affair of the barricades in January, 1960, the revolt of the generals in April, 1961, and the terrorism of the O.A.S. in 1962—were unsuccessful. Algeria became independent without the

French of Algeria being able to remain there and without France finding the economic benefits there that she had hoped to find. But, as seen by the Western world, the policy of "co-operation," which consists of giving to the Socialist regime of Ben Bella support of more than $300 million a year, has had the noteworthy consequence of preventing the creation of a second Cuba. If this situation continues, it will be regarded as a major success which has followed upon numerous minor failures.

Freed from the Algerian burden, Gaullist diplomacy suddenly showed that from this point on France was capable of astonishing flexibility and could now take the initiative. But before studying this initiative, it is essential first to discuss the framework in which it has developed.

The Fifth Republic inherited from the Fourth Republic three essential fundamentals of its policy:

1. The *Atlantic Pact,* which, thanks to the power of the United States, assures France of her security;

2. *Progression toward European economic unity* (though not political unity: the Fourth Republic did not know how to make of the Council of Europe an efficient organism, and furthermore she could not prevent the Community for European Defense from failing). This economic integration has justly been considered one of the factors of the present prosperity of the country;

3. *The increasing tendency toward decolonialization.*

These three elements have been maintained by the new regime. Decolonialization has been accelerated. European economic integration has benefitted from the vigor of the new leader, since it has surmounted the obstacle of the zone of free trade proposed by the English (December, 1958), resolved major portions of the agricultural problem (January, 1962, and December, 1963), risen above the psychological crisis provoked by the veto imposed by France to the English candidacy to the Common Market, and succeeded, to a certain degree, in presenting a common front

among the Six to the American propositions for the reciprocal lowering of customs tariffs called for by the Trade
Expansion Act of 1962.

Except for the case of the candidacy of Great Britain, a
problem which profoundly divided the men of the Fourth
Republic (the pro-English were in majority, though there
were also the anti-English, such as André Philip), the Fifth
Republic has left unchanged the fundamentals of the Fourth
Republic's policy toward economic integration. The difference, on the level of immediate goals, is that the men of
the Fourth Republic always presented economic integration
as a preface to eventual political integration, while General
de Gaulle has never hidden his scorn for "political" integration and his preference for a "Europe of states." This
is a basic difference on the level of ideas, but it must be
repeated that on the level of action there is a similarity
between the Fourth and Fifth Republics, since the Fourth
Republic did not undertake action in the realm of political
integration or, at least, did not succeed.

For the first fundamental—the Atlantic Pact—we notice
that official statements indicate an important difference
between the Fourth and the Fifth Republics, but that the
basic short-term policy remains the same. What General
de Gaulle disputes is not the Atlantic Alliance itself, but
its structure, NATO. As de Gaulle stated in his press conference on January 14, 1963, "The Atlantic Alliance exists.
As long as the Soviets threaten the world, this Alliance
must be maintained. France is an integral part of it. If
the free world were attacked, on the old or the new continent, France would take part in the common defense . . .
with all the means at her disposal."

Such statements, repeated in all of the General's press
conferences and in many of his speeches, suffice to render
mythical the fear of seeing France trigger a "reversal of
alliances" or leave NATO to head a neutralist bloc.

But once we have admitted the basic similarities of

Fourth and Fifth Republic policy, it is necessary to insist upon the total change of style and method, on the new atmosphere, and on the numerous actions which reveal a greater independence of action and a will distinct from that of France's major ally. In fact, it is apparent that this entirely new approach really changes nothing fundamental. For the present, and even for the immediate future, France remains completely faithful to the Alliance.

Let us briefly review the Gaullist actions which have created divergences and tension with the United States:

1. Refusal to integrate into NATO forces the tactical air units, the Mediterranean fleet in time of war, and the divisions repatriated from Algeria; the withdrawal of French naval officers from NATO positions;

2. The desire to create a national striking force, with the following corollaries:

    a) Refusal to accept the Nassau propositions for a "multinational" force and refusal to join a "multilateral" force;

    b) Refusal to sign the nuclear test-ban agreement of August, 1963; and

    c) Refusal to increase the number of conventional army divisions;

3. Refusal to admit Great Britain in the Common Market (January, 1963);

4. The proposition for the neutralization of Vietnam (late 1963); and

5. The *de jure* recognition of Communist China (February, 1964).

There is no doubt on any of these points. The irritation of the American government, of the press, and of public opinion has been so great that any number of other actions, which do not in the least imply divergence with American policy, have created ill-minded suspicions and fantastic interpretations. For example, the United States favors greater participation of European countries in commercial relations with Latin America and a greater contribution from these countries of financial aid. But when France offered a loan of $150 million to Mexico to finance the construction of petroleum refineries, American companies who probably had obtained the approval of their government made a more attractive offer to the Mexicans, thus rendering the French loan useless. When General de Gaulle visited Mexico he was accused—and often in rather impolite terms (see the statement of former President Truman) — of desiring to supplant American influence in that country. Yet when he had completed his stay and it was found that he had not made any important changes of policy, the weak means of action at France's disposal came under attack, and sarcasm, rather than gratitude, was directed at the General.

This poisoned atmosphere must be analyzed from two perspectives, that of motivation—why had this atmosphere been allowed to develop?—and that of effect—in what measure has it weakened the Atlantic Pact?

The Causes of Franco-American Tension

It is beyond doubt that the role of the General in the creation of this tension is of major importance, if not totally responsible.

Let us examine the tactical point of view. It is clear that, whatever his ultimate aims might be, the General had decided in 1962 that the time had come to "liberate" Europe, and especially France, from American leadership. His memory of President Roosevelt's inability to understand him is still very much alive.[1] He is probably less aware of his inability to understand President Roosevelt. He has

---

[1] I have studied this problem in a report entitled "Les grands alliés et la résistance extérieure française," for the Second Congress of the History of the Resistance, Milan, 1962.

always interpreted Roosevelt's actions, as well as the actions of his successors, as being a concentrated effort to establish and to perpetuate American influence in Europe, to build up and to maintain the levers of command. When President Kennedy, in his State of the Union address of January, 1962, proposed the development of an Atlantic community by stating that: "The emergence of the new Europe is being matched by the emergence of new ties across the Atlantic," it is without a doubt that the General saw in these words an attempt to maintain the leadership *in spite of* "the emergence of the new Europe." Thus, he declared his hostility toward "a huge Atlantic community dependent upon and under the direction of America which would soon absorb the European community." (January 14, 1963.) It is, moreover, remarkable that President Kennedy, doubtlessly influenced by Jean Monnet, rejected the term "Atlantic community" and used instead "Atlantic partnership" and "interdependence."

When General de Gaulle rejected the entry of Great Britain into the Common Market, it was largely because he regarded the "privileged ally" of the United States as a Trojan horse which the Americans would use to establish and maintain their dominating influence in Europe. And when President Kennedy, on January 1, 1963, declared that it was necessary to increase American leadership, General de Gaulle, as well as many Europeans, misread the sense of these words. In English, the word "leadership" can mean both "dominating role" and "capacity to lead the way." President Kennedy was certainly using the second meaning in his declaration, but de Gaulle interpreted the statement as a confirmation of President Kennedy's desire to dominate.

To eliminate domination, the best apparent method is to show that one will not be dominated, which one does by saying "no" or by taking independent initiatives without consulting the leader. In fact, the leader is not in the habit of consulting his allies. What Hans Morgenthau calls the American tendency toward "neoisolation"—we will deal with world affairs, but "on our own terms"—is an attitude frequently adopted by Americans. Having the means to make independent decisions, they too often have the tendency to think that these decisions are good for others as well, and merely inform them of these decisions out of politeness after the decisions have been made. To use the same method in the opposite direction is a good way to show Americans that one is not dependent on them.

General de Gaulle has both used and abused this "tactic of saying no." A summary analysis brings to light the following elements of this tactic:

a) It is certainly valid that the weaker partner in an unbalanced alliance can sometimes show the stronger partner that their interests are not necessarily the same. "Neither the French-American friendship, nor the Alliance, could be questioned, nor are they. But it is true that in the presence of the problems now facing the two countries, their policies are not always in agreement. We both must adapt ourselves to this new situation." (January 14, 1963.)

To use occasionally the "no" is probably a better tactic than that which consists of continually saying "yes," and is even better than trying to convince "big brother" directly that his policy must be changed. General Wedemeyer criticized the British generals in lively terms for acting in this fashion during the war.

b) Furthermore, there is nothing inherently wrong with forcing the major partner to reconsider his policy. Complete or partial failures of American foreign policy in the past few years have been numerous: Cuba, the Alliance for Progress, Panama, Laos, and Vietnam are examples. The rigidity of the policy with regard to China or the inefficiency of the economic reprisal method and the control of exportations toward Communist countries seem to indicate that a profound reappraisal is called for. Senator Mike Mansfield has been won over to the policy of neutralization for Vietnam, and more recently, Senator Fulbright has proposed a major revision of the international policies of the United States. (March 26, 1964.)

c) On the other hand, the United States has the right to be irritated when the initiatives of its ally endangers a situation for which it bears the responsibility, a situation which, as the United States is aware, this ally cannot deal with itself. Perhaps it is intrinsically good to propose the neutralization of Vietnam. (We will not take up this question here.) But to do so publicly is to weaken the morale of the men who are fighting against the Viet Cong.

d) Moreover, the initiatives of the weaker ally can be taken only because this ally knows that it is protected by the American deterrent. While it is rare for nations to show their gratitude and their good intentions, it appears revolting to many Americans that France takes these initiatives and uses the policy of the systematic "no" precisely because she feels protected by those to whom she says no.

All of this is very much in accord with the taste of General de Gaulle for isolation and with the idea—magnificently expressed in his memoirs—that he is condemned to be alone. Solitude in action implies little desire to "consult." If one is to concede that Europe's role in the Alliance must increase and that Americans must understand this legitimate aspiration for increased independence, it is evident that Europeans, less through courtesy than through a well-conceived sense of their own interests, must consult their major ally before taking the initiative, in order, at least, to avoid embarrassing him.

It is probable that another French president—Gaston Defferre, for example—would follow essentially the same lines as General de Gaulle. But it is also probable that his "style" would be different. "When one says one is not in agreement, and why one is not in agreement, the Ameri-

cans understand and admit it. What they do not understand is that they are not consulted." (Gaston Defferre,
Le Monde, March 29–30, 1964.)

The Consequences of Franco-American Tension

After his magistral victory in the Cuban affair of October, 1962, President Kennedy defended more strongly than
ever the idea that the West must remain united in opposition to the divided Communist camp. The abrupt refusal
given by General de Gaulle concerning the Nassau proposal
and the entrance of Great Britain into the Common Market appeared to him, as well as to many Americans, as
a form of treason. This problem is, however, more complex than it first appears.

If the socialist camp—China, Russia, and Yugoslavia—is
divided, even for rivalries which are essentially national
ones, this division is represented immediately on the ideological level and thus assumes serious proportions. A so-
ciological doctrine like Marxism-Leninism which gives a
monistic explanation for history can accept neither heresy
nor plurality. On the contrary, the Western camp's basic
principles originate not from an ideology but from liberty,
from the possibility that each citizen has of choosing his
own ideology. Each state in the Western world is essentially pluralistic. Relations between Western states cannot
be ideological relations. Thus, the only friction between
them is caused by conflicts of national interest. If these
states are allies, it is because their common interests are
of greater value than their differences. That these differences exist is, to quote de Gaulle, "nothing that is essential
or fundamentally disturbing or even surprising."

While the socialist camp is profoundly shaken by internal
dissension, the Western camp should feel only minor effects of such dissension. It would really suffer if this dissension assumed such forms that it could destroy the Alli-

ance. But if the Alliance endures, these differences must, in principle, be only nominal, and might, in the long run, provoke fruitful change.

The danger lies in the fact that American opinion and many American leaders, accustomed by the Cold War to Manichaean interpretations like those of President Truman and John Foster Dulles that there is no middle ground between black and white, have constructed not an ideology but a counterideology which, when pushed to extremes, produces McCarthyism or the John Birch Society. Naturally, the fundamental wisdom of this great people and its democratic system prevent extreme consequences. But the danger, at least as seen from abroad, is ever present. This counterideology is *anticommunism*.

In an article entitled "The Impotence of American Power," Hans Morgenthau has put his finger on the source of the weakness. "Our impotence," he writes, "is aggravated and rendered irreparable by our commitment to anti-Communism as the overriding objective of our foreign policy. For most of our allies, anti-Communism is at best incidental to concrete national objectives and at worst irrelevant to them." [2]

This statement means that the Americans, having fought communism because it directly menaced their national interest during the period of Stalin's provocations, continue to be guided by the essential principle of anticommunism, even though the Communist danger lessens. If there is an intensification of the Cold War, then the allies will faithfully close ranks. But if the Cold War becomes less important, because the U.S.S.R. is slowly but steadily abandoning its revolutionary expansionism, or because the American deterrent is effectively on guard in Europe, then diverging national interests reappear. If we are on the brink—as we were over Cuba in October, 1962—the allies declare complete solidarity. But if there is no longer any

[2] *Commentary*, November 1963, pp. 384–86.

brink, if the allies become aware, like Senator Fulbright, that the Castro regime must be considered "a distasteful nuisance but not an intolerable danger," then the specific interests reappear and the allies sell buses and trucks to Castro. All the allies do this, not just Gaullist France but also the "privileged ally," the United Kingdom.

Thus, because the United States, supported by a slow historical process, has pushed the danger back, the divergences among free states reappear. It is impossible that it could be otherwise. The friendly allies who say "yes" and the arrogant ally who says "no" are equal here. But these divergences—sources of weakness for the East—are, on the contrary, signs of strength and of health for the West.

But there is a limit to this type of reasoning of which General de Gaulle is not, perhaps, aware. Even if there is no weakening of the Alliance in an *objective* sense, there is a weakening if the strongest ally, the United States, *subjectively* believes in this weakening. This irritation might even lead to a bitter exchange of blows. Absurd as this might sound, the possibility must not be excluded. The United States might go so far as to practice the "agonizing reappraisal" with which Dulles menaced France in December, 1953, in the eventuality of the CED failure. The United States could, then, break the Alliance, or force France to break it, in the course of such an emotional reaction. In this regard the wisdom of President Kennedy provided a guarantee which we cannot be sure of with his successor. Kennedy refused the alternative of violent reprisals against General de Gaulle's attack of January 14, 1963, on his "Grand Design." "What we would regard as a serious blow," the late President countered, "would be, however, a division between the United States and Europe, [the] inability of Europe and the United States to coordinate their policies to deal with this great challenge." (Press conference, February 7, 1963.)

So the real danger lies not within the framework of the Alliance, but in the possibility that the provocation may be so great on one side and that the irritation may be so great on the other side that the Alliance will break. Even if he is sometimes right, objectively, in his criticism, it is thus wrong for General de Gaulle to irritate carelessly his powerful and indispensable ally. Once again it is apparent that the real problem is how to establish a *system of consultation*. It is because they have too greatly minimized the importance of this process in dealing with their allies, who are recovering their power and slowly achieving economic prosperity, that Americans have created the false impression that they wanted to remain the leaders merely because of their desire for power. They thus provoked haughty displays of independence on the part of their most prideful ally. Conversely, it is because he has also refused this consultation that General de Gaulle has threatened the Alliance. If it is only for reasons of protocol that President Johnson and the General refuse to meet, i.e., to consult, then their decisions serve to weaken the Alliance. But this same Alliance is not weakened by manifestations of national interest which are, of course, different for each nation. *What is really necessary is that co-ordination by unilateral decisions originating in the United States be replaced by co-ordination through an effective consultative process.* This process could be created if statesmen succeed in dominating their emotions and in not sacrificing reality on the altar of impassioned public opinion. It must be repeated, in summary, that *the danger lies not in the divergences, but in isolationist attitudes.*

Long-Range Views: Gaullist Strategy

On the tactical level, in the short- and middle-range perspective, we have noticed the development of a certain tension which has been intensified by the absence of means of consultation. But the possibility remains that the long-range perspectives for world events on either side of the Atlantic are fundamentally different. It is necessary for us to examine here the information we have relating to the overall Gaullist strategy.

We may consider the key of the Gaullist system to be the conviction that *nations will outlive ideologies.* The necessary corollary to this conviction is that a policy must strive to weaken ideologies rather than to attack them directly. Moreover, the unit of the "nation" is a complex and varied collectivity which can be protected from the "fermentation of dispersion" only by "great undertakings." (Charles de Gaulle, *L'Appel*, p. 1.) The nation, then, must be realistic rather than ideologic. To recognize Communist China is to recognize a nation of 700 million inhabitants who must be heard. To refuse this recognition because China is a Communist country is to close one's eyes to reality and to yield to the "counterideology" we have mentioned above.

There are abundant proofs for the conviction that nations will outlive ideologies. Little by little, Russia will discover that she is a nation. "Without a doubt," stated the General, "Soviet Russia is discovering that no matter what happens, she is still Russia, a white, European nation, the conqueror of part of Asia, who is endowed with land, mines, factories, and other wealth, and confronted by the yellow multitudes which populate China, innumerable and miserable, indestructible and ambitious." (November, 1959.) But China herself is "presently" under the yoke of the terrible Communist dictatorship. (January, 1964.) Alfred Grosser has correctly stressed the importance of this word "presently." In the short run, China is Communist and is thus a potential enemy (a situation which in no way prevents one from following the European tradition, and the pre-Wilsonian tradition in America, in recognizing her because she exists). In the long run, China will always be China.

We can sum up from this analysis, then, that the Atlantic Pact is "presently" indispensable. But with the disappearance of Communist ideology the necessity for the pact will also disappear, and the free play of diplomacy between nations might once again be manifest, in the fashion of pre-1914 Europe.

That the world of the future must be, "by the very nature of things being as they are," a world of nations, implies that the genesis of this future would be prepared as of now. And the basis for this preparation is that a *crystallization* of the present world be avoided. Here are the four principal components of this task:

1. The avoidance of a global accord between the two major powers which would divide the world and give each power a monopoly of control in its sphere;

2. The avoidance of any stabilization of the Atlantic Alliance in the form of an Atlantic community which would perpetuate American leadership;

3. The encouragement of the "Third World" to maintain its independence of either power bloc; and

4. The augmentation of all available means of power for France and, by extension, for Europe, in such a way that Europe can fill the role for which she is worthy in the future development of history.

1. One of the essential ideas of President Kennedy, an idea which doubtless will assure him of an eminent place in history, was that it was possible to effect a *rapprochement* with the Soviet Union not by yielding ground on the important issues but by continually seeking new negotiations. In this way a system of "tacit bargaining" found its place in the gap of reciprocal mistrust which separates the United States and the Soviet Union. By this new system, the two gigantic partners attempt to show that through a realistic dialogue a minimum of confidence between them

can be established and that a faint glimmer of hope for a general *rapprochement* can be seen. Premier Khrushchev tried to see how far he could go in the Cuban affair. But when he discovered that he had passed the limit tolerated by the United States, he showed that bargaining was possible by the promptness of his retreat.

The Test Ban Treaty of August, 1963, objectively insignificant, continued in the same direction and has great subjective importance. And it must not be overlooked that on several occasions Premier Khrushchev has placed the "superior interests of humanity" over the immediate stake of the revolution.

There is nothing in this perspective of "peaceful coexistence" which is contrary to Gaullist ideas, since the idea of a real *rapprochement* of the East and West is basic to the General's concept of the melting-away of ideologies. On the contrary, however, de Gaulle might be unequivocally opposed to such a *rapprochement* if it takes the form of a *U.S.S.R.-United States understanding* rather than an *East-West understanding*. Under the pretext that the "balance of terror" is working well and that the dissemination of nuclear capability is an inherent evil, the two major powers might agree to hold this monopoly for themselves and thus exclude the possibility for lesser states or even for Europe to attain eventually a position of *grandeur*.

The recognition of Communist China and the refusal of France to sign the test ban treaty are, evidently, explained by fear of such a policy. It is necessary that the present bipolar structure of the world be replaced by a multipolar system. To quote C. L. Sulzberger (*New York Times,* February 17, 1964), "The U.S. and the U.S.S.R. remain unchallenged as superpowers but their strength is more military and potential than political and actual. They are unable to prevent their ideological clients from acting on their own. They can only protect them in a crisis." He continues, under the title "De Gaulle's Role," on February

23, 1964: ". . . it became clear that neither of the Big Two would willingly go to nuclear war with the other. The corollary has been that the Allies feel that they need no longer put aside their national interests out of deference to the United States."

2. The Atlantic Alliance is an imperative necessity in a world where communism remains on the offensive. It assures Europe of the protection of the United States for years to come. On this point, de Gaulle certainly does not share the ideas of General Gallois which affirm that American protection no longer exists. How could France gradually develop her striking force if she did not have American protection? In spite of American disapproval, it is the United States' deterrent which allows France to produce her own arsenal.

In this perspective, Gaullist policy is very much like that of the British, except that the latter have a ten-year head start and the benefits gained by the communication of American secrets.

3. The "Third World" is a term describing an agglomeration comprised of existing nation-states (Latin America) and of states in the process of formation that are destined to regroup and evolve as they seek their identity, often at the price of great suffering and strain. For these states, neutralism has a special value. In order to prevent them from sliding into the Communist camp, it is better to encourage the neutralist tendency than to create necessarily unstable alliances with them. It should be noted that French aid toward these countries, notably in Africa, is only secondarily concerned with military bases (Reggane, and In-Ekker in the Algerian Sahara, and Mers-el-Kebir, for a fifteen-year period, in Algeria) and military co-operation. French aid as a percentage of gross national product is quite substantial: 2.41 per cent of the GNP, as compared with the American figure of 0.9 per cent of GNP and the British figure of 1.17 per cent of GNP. Most

French aid comes under the heading of "co-operation agreements," which are in no way alliances. Some of it goes into programs such as the Common Market-Africa Association, which brings into the system France's five partners in the Common Market and the proposition of a large-scale stabilization plan for the raw-material markets. (Speech by M. Giscard d'Estaing at the G.A.T.T. conference in March, 1964.)

General de Gaulle has consistently suggested the status of neutrality for Southeast Asia and particularly for the area of former French Indo-China. France, which has never hesitated in its support for Prince Souvanna Phouma in Laos, and has disapproved of the American attempt to establish a pro-Western government with Prince Boun Oum and General Phoumi, was pleased to see President Kennedy's acceptance of the idea of neutralization in April, 1961. And it is France that is considered by Prince Norodom Sihanouk of Cambodia as the sole hope for maintaining his country's neutrality. America is to him a potential enemy which supports Thailand and South Vietnam, the traditional rivals of Cambodia. Finally, General de Gaulle, in what were perhaps inopportune circumstances, stated that the solution to the Vietnam problem lay not in an impossible military victory but in a neutralization of the two Vietnams, thus implying an agreement with China, the possibility of which remains to be seen.

In addition to these concrete instances, it is possible to find even another type of maneuver in Gaullist strategy. Since France and England have almost concluded the process of decolonization, the leftist leaders of the new countries, under the inspiration of the U.S.S.R. and, especially, of China, have directed their attacks against economic "neocolonialism." Although France is not immune to these attacks, they have been primarily directed at the United States. The "Conference of Afro-Asian Solidarity," which was held in Algiers in March, 1964, "took for its prime target," according to *Le Monde,* March 29–30, 1964, "the American policy toward the 'Third World.'" In Latin America, "Yankee phobia" strikes the eye of even the least informed observer. General de Gaulle, by his "tactic of no" toward the United States, by his will to independence, by his encouragement of neutralism, and even by his recognition of Communist China, has been assuring his popularity in many parts of the world. His welcome in Mexico, the request of Mgr. Makarios for his mediation in Cyprus, his correspondence with Prince Norodom Sihanouk of Cambodia, and the unexpected visit of President Ben Bella of Algeria to Paris are all signs of this popularity.

Is this a superficial popularity? Probably it is, but as irritating as de Gaulle's popularity has become for the United States, it is based upon anti-Americanism which is not superficial. General de Gaulle increases his popularity at the expense of his major ally, and it is not surprising that this ally finds the procedure thoroughly disagreeable.

If one approaches the problem calmly, it is evident that de Gaulle's policy really serves American interests as well: it opens a breach in the ill-conceived Manichaean system in which one is either for or against the United States. Between pro-Castroism and pro-Americanism, this policy has created the new possibility of being pro-Western without being "sold to Washington." Between the United States and China, this policy opens a third path for Cambodia.

In any case, this policy serves to demonstrate that a power of medium strength, and even a small power (for there are singular resemblances between Gaullist views and those of Marshal Tito regarding the Third World) is capable of playing a role disproportionate with its forces and the actual means at its disposal.

In sum, General de Gaulle is evidently trying to neutralize the Third World wherever possible and to assimilate this neutralization with independence—desired all over the world—which is the best means of preventing these countries from "sliding" into the Communist camp. The only doubt which this policy raises—and it is an important one—is that France does not really have the means to follow it up all over the world. Her economic aid is limited, and French opinion has subjected this question to increasingly thorough examination. (See Raymond Cartier's articles and the book by Edouard Bonnefous, *Les milliards qui s'envolent.*) Her commerce with the new countries is, in general, too small in volume, and it cannot be greatly increased. France's military aid is inconsequential. So even if the idea is a good one, the force of the idea is not sufficient in itself unless it is supported by powerful material means.

The only way to develop this policy more fully would be to pass from the French to the European level of action. But this change would necessitate the interest of France's economic partners, and these partners are hardly interested. With regard to this policy of neutralism the tacit approval of the United States would also be necessary. But the State Department does not seem to have appreciated the virtues of such a scheme, and Congress, evidently, has entirely different views.

Whatever the possibilities may be, the Gaullist strategy on this point is clear. The Third World, which is currently a stake in the game of world politics, must play its own role. It can do this only by remaining independent of the two giants.

4. In the world of the future, where nations will dominate ideologies, what is the role of France? How must she establish her relationship to Europe? What is General de Gaulle's position on this question? And in what measure does he represent the inclinations of French opinion? [3]

---

[3] For what follows I am using, in an adapted version, the conclusions of my article "La France et la Collaboration Atlantique," *Revue economique et sociale,* Lausanne, September, 1963, pp. 65–78.

It is necessary to see how he envisages the European community. In appearance there is a contradiction—repeatedly stressed, most recently by Alfred Grosser [4]—between his will to bring about total economic integration and his conception of a "Europe of States." He has even renounced the idea of "integration" on the political level, thus causing the resignation of his M.R.P. cabinet ministers. But this contradiction is more apparent than real if we compare his conception of the present, of "reality," with his conception of future developments which are bound to result from "the nature of things."

The present is, of course, marked by the predominance of national states over internationalism. The General has stated that, in spite of the

> . . . sirens which sing to us the sweetness of renunciation . . . there is not a chance that, by following the easy path, we will allow France to disappear. It is for this reason that, if the union of Western Europe . . . is one of the desired goals of our external action, we have no desire to dissolve ourselves. Any system which would convey our sovereignty to an international authority would be incompatible with the rights and duties of the French Republic.

This would be an "abdication" which "would inevitably lead to external subjugation."

And for the future? "It is necessary," de Gaulle said at Givet on April 23, 1963, "to contribute in the most direct manner toward bringing about the union of Europe. This ideal is already realized on the economic level. It must be the same on the political level. It must be brought about wisely and reasonably, with consideration for realities and also for sentiment."

Thus it is in the perspective of a distant future that the General speaks of a Europe extending "from the Atlantic

---

[4] "General de Gaulle and the Foreign Policy of the Fifth Republic," *International Affairs,* April, 1963, pp. 198–213.

to the Urals," a formula which has provoked the fruitless spilling of a great deal of ink. Those commentators who have evoked the possibility of a "reversal of alliances" seem to have followed their emotional fury rather than the texts. In fact, few Western political leaders have expressed in harsher terms their attitude toward Soviet "tyranny," toward the bloc which has "ambitions of domination at every moment," and toward leaders who "want neither liberty nor equality nor fraternity." No one has a firmer attitude toward West Berlin. No one more vigorously applauded the success of President Kennedy in the Cuban affair. But, if his attitude must be firm, it is "until the internal evolution [of the Soviet Union], its inevitable humanization, leads it first to a warming of relations, and then, possibly to an understanding with free men such as us." [5] But the evolution of the future changes nothing of the present, and in the present the U.S.S.R. is the "potential enemy."

The attitude of General de Gaulle must be seen in the following perspective:

a) Although favorable toward the economic integration of Europe, he rejected the candidacy of Great Britain for entry into the Common Market, primarily on economic grounds. André Philip, a political adversary, wrote in *Le Monde,* April 17, 1963, that

> . . . by claiming minimal duties for some products and thus reopening competition with the rates established by the Community, by wanting to reserve for the Commonwealth markets which were comparable to European markets, and by demanding steps and delays which would have menaced a common agricultural policy which was barely in use, our English friends have shown that they are less interested in participating at the core of a federalized Europe than in the enlargement of this Europe in a greater zone of free trade.

[5] April 23, 1963, Châlons-sur-Marne.

b) Because of his hostility toward an "Atlantic community," General de Gaulle rejected British admission for political reasons as well. In his eyes, Great Britain had too faithfully accepted American directives at Nassau. Held back by the Commonwealth, she was also held back by the United States. She would be America's Trojan horse in a European community. The General seems to have minimized the fact that the British as well as the French have only moderate sympathy for American leadership, and that large sectors of British public opinion had envisaged entry into the Common Market as a means of assuring Great Britain of more independence from her powerful ally.

c) To these political reasons, which are acceptable, can perhaps be added some reasons which are less acceptable. While it is absurd, as we have stated, to think in terms of a reversal of alliances, or even of Gaullist "neutralism," it is very likely that General de Gaulle is seeking for France a sort of "leadership" of Europe. Obviously, he has never admitted this. We know that the English translation of his memoirs rendered the word *sécurité* (in Europe) as "primacy," which is an obvious error. Nevertheless, the goal which he has proposed, and on which he insists, is the *grandeur* of France; he has consecrated his life to returning this defeated and humiliated country to its proper rank. While admitting that France cannot be as powerful as the United States or the U.S.S.R., it is clear that he aspires to make of her the first-ranking of the medium-strength powers.

He exposes his thesis luminously on page 1 of the first volume of his *Mémoires de Guerre*: "France cannot be France without *grandeur*." Why *grandeur*? Because the French people can overcome its basic tendency toward disunity only by participating in "great undertakings." The art of governing consists of providing for the people great undertakings which are worthy and capable of creating enthusiasm. In 1945–46 it was the transformation of the colonies into the "French Union." Since 1958, it is "decolonialization" and "economic expansion." Both these terms describe "great undertakings."

Thus we can grasp the profound methods of the General. Since France, because of her size, cannot achieve superior rank by herself, external supports must be found, in Europe, in the former colonies, and, perhaps later, in Latin America.

Now that its decolonization has been completed, France finds itself, among all the countries of the European Common Market, to have the greatest flexibility in matters of foreign policy. Germany is burdened with her division and with the Berlin problem. Italy is locked in the Mediterranean and has no outside bases of support. She has not even been able to get a linguistic foothold in Africa. Only the United Kingdom has a flexibility which is comparable to France's; hence the distrust created by its candidacy for Market membership.

If France could become the spokesman for the Common Market, the leader of this group, she would be propelled by this massive support toward the front ranks. Naturally such a policy would rouse the suspicions of her partners, who, if they felt that a leader was necessary, would want an incontestably first-class power. But the possibility cannot be overlooked that Chancellor Adenauer—and he alone in Germany—did implicitly accept French "leadership" in the summer of 1958, as an exchange for complete French support in the Berlin matter. The diplomatic victory against the British concept of a zone of free trade at the end of the same year was a victory for France, won with German support. And as for the famous Franco-German treaty, which was signed on a date coincidental with the "anti-Anglo-Saxon" press conference on January 14, 1963, it can be interpreted as the seal on a fine and meritorious reconciliation—in which case it is enthusiastically regarded

—or it can be seen as the consecration of French leadership, thus provoking the indignation of Italian, Belgian, Dutch, and even German public opinion. It is all really a question of psychology, for the treaty is politically insignificant.

Another benefit from the completion of decolonialization is that France can now be supported in her foreign policy by many African states where French is spoken either officially or by custom. In this domain the General's ideas never varied. His actions show his extraordinary suppleness, as he tried every possible formula to obtain this support. In 1958, it was the "constitutional" community, in which France assumed responsibility of this group's foreign affairs; in 1960, the *de facto* community of independent states; then the "African and Malagasy Union" with its privileged status; and finally the doctrine of "co-operation" has been established, a concept preferred to that of "association."

This system has been highly valuable from the linguistic point of view. At United Nations and UNESCO meetings 33–38 per cent of the speeches are given in French. This figure, close behind the English percentage, proves that French has regained its former status as an international language. From the political point of view, the General's scorn for the U.N., the "machine"—another source of irritation for the Americans—prevents him from taking advantage of the pro-French bloc. On the whole, the policy of "co-operation" has produced two political results: it has permitted France to use certain military bases, and it has assured France of almost certain international support. In exchange, France pays many of the bills for these new nations.

The United States approves of France's policy of aid for underdeveloped countries and regards her as a good ally in this domain, especially because the "African and Malagasy Union," even in its new form, is clearly pro-Western, and the other countries which receive French aid—Morocco and Algeria—are prevented from sliding entirely into the anti-Western camp, although they are neutralists and members of the "Casablanca Group," because of the advantages offered them by the co-operation policy.

The policy of General de Gaulle can thus be called a "policy of double support," European and African. His grandiose projects foresee that the *grandeur* of France must, "by the very nature of things," result from the combined elements of the independent striking force, European (primarily German) support, African support, and—perhaps—Latin American support.

Conclusion: French Opinion Faced with Dreams and Reality

If our interpretation is fairly accurate, as the texts quoted above seem to indicate, then the confrontation of de Gaulle's program and Kennedy's "Grand Design" is indeed violent. This is not so because General de Gaulle is becoming a neutralist, but because his aim is directed at American leadership. The group of the late President's advisers which has stayed on in the Johnson Administration, for all its brilliance, does not seem to grasp the fact that Europe's new economic situation makes it continually more difficult for Europeans to accept this leadership. One might say, by way of hypothesis, that there exists a great economic potential which utterly destroys the comforting illusion held by too many Americans that Europe will always rely on them for security and that the United States will maintain her monopoly of authority. It is naturally enough quite distressing, even for the idealists, to move down from the position of uncontested leader to the role of a mere partner. But no trick of vocabulary, including the ambiguous term "Atlantic community," can block this process.

In his pursuance of this policy General de Gaulle is more or less supported by French public opinion. This is understandable, since France, more than most countries, has particularly suffered from "humiliation." The French Institute of Public Opinion has clearly demonstrated that, in spite of the relative indifference of French opinion to foreign policy, France wishes above all to be "independent," and not be "humiliated." [6] This phenomenon, with certain nuances, goes beyond the frontiers of France. It manifested itself in Germany, when General de Gaulle provoked a large and enthusiastic response by recalling that the Germans are "a great people"—something which no one had told them for a long time. In England, it manifested itself in the horror and humiliation of a large portion of the populace as being a "brilliant second," [7] and elsewhere as well.

But if General de Gaulle has been the spokesman of this profound hope, the impassioned irritation which he has provoked shows that he has run up against other equally profound hopes.

We will overlook those of the "Kennedy team" and the American press. It is always unpleasant to watch the collapse of a "Grand Design," one conforming, what is more, to the classic lines of American foreign policy.

The irritation of the British is more interesting to analyze. It has two parts. First, the irritation is the product of the humiliation of a country which, after fighting valiantly in World War II, had to put up with two of the General's "no's," at the end of 1958 and in January, 1963. Secondly, the irritation is the expression of opinion which believes that the French President has committed an error. The United Kingdom had a choice between continuing the unpopular policy of being a "brilliant second" or entering the European Economic Community. The General rejected

---

[6] *Sondages*, October, 1958.

[7] Morgenthau, "The Impotence of American Power."

the entry of the "brilliant second" without understanding that it was precisely in order to cease being the "brilliant second" that England had posed its candidacy. Hence Mr. Macmillan's thesis: France rejected the English candidacy not because an economic *rapprochement* was impossible (this being the thesis of M. Couve de Murville) , but because this *rapprochement* was, indeed, highly likely. Thus the French motives were not economic, but political.

The irritation of France's Common Market partners stems from similar reasons, with the exception of the Dutch and some Germans, whose economic interests were at stake. For the Italians, the combination of the refusal to admit England and the signature of the Franco-German treaty revealed a desire for hegemony on the part of France which Italy quite naturally did not desire.

In France there has not been much actual irritation. The temporary decline in the General's popularity (60–65 per cent approved of his policies in November, 1962; this figure fell to 55 per cent in January and 42 per cent in March, but rose to 50 per cent again in April, 1963) was caused by social tension rather than by foreign policy. But the "pro-European" and "neorealist" elite of the country, along with a good portion of the population, was rudely shocked. On the one hand, the tone of the General's January 14, 1963, press conference was unacceptable. Even if Europe has, in the words of Walter Hallstein, "passed the point of no return," the members of the European community have a psychological need for a certain mutual courtesy and confidence in their dealings. This confidence has been badly shaken by the General.

On the other hand, de Gaulle's concern for "grandeur" and "leadership" is not shared by the majority of French opinion. This majority is not inherently hostile to the General's concepts, but it becomes hostile to them when the whims of leadership delay the construction of a united Europe. And whatever may be its long-range consequences, the January 14 press conference has turned out to be a significant delaying factor.

Several concepts of a "united Europe" are current in France today, determined by the ideologies and interests of those who sponsor them. One of these views, sponsored by Jean Monnet, foresees the creation of a European political entity including England and associated in "partnership" with the United States. (Monnet, like most Frenchmen, rejects President Kennedy's vague "Atlantic community.") Another concept of a united Europe, sponsored by more intransigent Europeans like André Philip, excludes England from the picture until she has made her "trip to Canossa." The common bond among these criticisms of Gaullist policy is that they all go further than the General on the matter of European political unity, and thus suggest, as an imperative condition of such unity, that all ideas of French leadership be abandoned.

Finally, we return to the question of the national striking force. Even after eliminating the arguments of the demagogues who claim that military expenditures are the major stumbling block to social progress, we find that the average Frenchman does not have faith in the value of a purely national deterrent. But rather than favoring a rapid halt in its development, both semi-Gaullists such as Pierre Pflimlin and members of the opposition like Maurice Faure foresee the prospect of "Europeanizing" the deterrent. And so we run up against the necessity of European unity and British participation once again. After all, it is rather hard to conceive of the Europeanization of the deterrent without a fusion of Franco-British forces and, consequently, without the creation of a unified political power.

The strength of Gaullism is that it seeks to emancipate Europe; its weakness is that it is repugnant, for the sake of France, to unifying Europe. His strength also comes from flattering the desire of "independence" all over the world; its weakness from his ambition to make France a

leading power, thus sacrificing the noble Wilsonian principle of the equality of all states. Finally, he may have a
very active foreign policy only because France is protected
by the American deterrent. What would happen if that policy, by irritating the U.S. beyond acceptable limits, would
induce them to revert to isolationism? It is not bad to
demonstrate publicly, by action, that Western foreign policy should not be crystallized, that the West can and must
be more dynamic. But it has not to be done at the expense
of the minimum of cohesion which an alliance demands.

Prospects and Designs for the West

by

Jacques Freymond*

(Translated from the French by Miss Elizabeth Stabler)

For several years, the attention of Western observers has been focused on the evolution of the socialist system toward polycentrism and on the political consequences flowing therefrom. More recently, efforts have been made to calculate the effects of growing tension in relations between the U.S.S.R. and China. By contrast, certain blatant manifestations of the French will for independence have been necessary in order to discover within the Western Alliance the ever more perceptible pressures of centrifugal forces which are braking progress toward European integration and even placing Atlantic ties in doubt.

This tendency of the Western world toward a "polycentrism," which is natural enough in societies calling themselves "pluralist," does not find its only expression in the behavior of General de Gaulle, who is charged a bit too readily with all sins. He who observes with attention the reactions provoked even in France by some of de Gaulle's

---

* *Jacques Freymond:* Professor of international history and Director of the Graduate Institute of International Studies, Geneva.

criticisms aimed at "Anglo-Saxons" is tempted to conclude
that the President of the Republic is not as isolated from
the French nation as it might seem and that, among his
fellow   citizens,   some   of   her   adversaries   see   some
virtue in his affirmation of French independence. The
disappearance of General de Gaulle would not necessarily lead to modifications in French foreign policy conforming to the views and wishes of partisans of European
union or of Atlantic community.

The action of centrifugal forces has been apparent in
still other forms and in other places. Thus, in Great Britain, the Conservative government defends with as much
conviction as the French its right to an independent nuclear force, while the Labour Party opposition favors formulas for unilateral disarmament and "disengagement"
which are just as contrary to Washington's ideas of a military policy for the West. Europe herself—why not recognize it?—is divided. The creation of the European Free
Trade Association not only reflects divergences of opinion
on economic policy; it also implies rejection of the formulas of integration defined by the Treaty of Rome, and
thereby, whether one wishes it or not, takes on political
significance. The members of EFTA are not opposed to
European co-operation; they are opposed to a certain conception of continental organization which for them does
not respect that diversity which is the force of Europe and
one of the sources of its influence. Here, moreover, they
find themselves partially in agreement with de Gaulle's
criticism of a policy that seeks to integrate that which can
be co-ordinated with just as much efficacy.

Divergences in views capable of compromising Western
unity of action are also apparent within nations. It would
be wrong to underestimate the importance of the tension in
Germany which arises from the division of the German
people into two rival states. One cannot ignore the continuing debate over denuclearization within the Scandinavian

countries, nor the importance of the problems that Sweden's policy of neutrality and the ambiguous situation of Finland pose for Denmark and Norway as nations committed to the Atlantic Alliance. In Italy, opposition to a policy of Atlantic collaboration does not lie only in the socialist left and in a powerful Communist party which is cleverly guided by a leader who seems to orient it toward tranquilizing Titoist formulas. The opposition has also found a place in the heart of the government, where it cannot be discounted by the Christian Democratic majority. Portugal, isolated within the Atlantic Alliance, is struggling with a double crisis brought on by decolonization and the aging of the regime. Finally, Greece and Turkey, the two eastern bastions of NATO, find themselves face to face in the Cyprus conflict, both led by governments unsure of their power and uncertain of their policies.

Thus the bipolar system, elaborated under the double influence of the Communist challenge and the development of nuclear arsenals, seems to be dissolving. Perhaps, moreover, it was only a myth, the product of a conceptual effort which lost touch with reality. The increasing militarization of political thought, the ever more marked tendency in the West to constrain changing reality within models and theories, brought about an unsuspected intellectual impoverishment, a dulling of sensibilities, a decline in the intuitive faculties so essential to the practice of the political art.

The awakening is that much more painful. It is not only in the East, within the Socialist system to which one had attached once and for all the label of monolithic, that centrifugal forces are at work. It is not only Soviet hegemony which is menaced, and menaced in spite of the formidable and in some respects decisive trump conferred by nuclear power. In the West also, where it was thought that a more liberal, more open, and hence flexible system of international relations had been elaborated, the crisis of

American leadership poses a problem of very real gravity. Because this crisis does not arise from the fact that the leader has lost the power or the will to assume his responsibilities. It is a result of economic and political transformations which have come about within the Western world as well as in its relations with the Third World; it is reflected in a growing impatience with the disciplines imposed by the Alliance which bind together most of the Western countries, and in a questioning of proffered guidelines. In the final analysis, the crisis has to do with the very nature of American leadership.

In these conditions, it is rather difficult to clarify the perspectives.

Some have been occasionally tempted to envisage a spectacular reversal of alliances. The elliptical formula of a Europe extending from "the Atlantic to the Urals" and the recognition of Red China by the French government have invited the thought that de Gaulle was deliberately accepting the risk of a rupture of the Atlantic Alliance in order to engage France in those political maneuvers reserved only to great powers. This hypothesis does not take account of the very plain declarations made by the President of the French Republic or by his close collaborators, nor of the attitude he has adopted in certain specific cases when the interests of the West have been at stake. It is, moreover, an oversimplified explanation of a policy that is at once simple and subtle. Remember, on more than one occasion, General de Gaulle has underlined the importance he assigns to an Alliance which he considers necessary. If he has proposed its reorganization to take account of changes in the situation of the Western world, he has not contested its utility. Moreover, he has always stated very clearly what separates him from the Soviet Union and Communist China. Let us recall his reflections on the latter country during his press conference of January 31, 1964, when he evoked the means employed to spur progress in China: "As is always the case in Communist systems, realizations are accompanied by terrible popular suffering, ruthless constraint of the masses, immense losses and waste in goods, the suppression and decimation of innumerable human values." And later he added: "Is it necessary to say that for our part there is nothing in this decision that represents the slightest approbation for the political system which is at present dominant in China?"

Positive declarations on the Atlantic Alliance and friendship with the United States are not lacking. Expressing himself in the most categorical terms, General de Gaulle devoted a long passage in his press conference of July 30, 1963, to these subjects: "The Atlantic Alliance is an elemental necessity," he said. And he went on to remark:

> Thus if, once more, there are differences between Washington and Paris over the organization and functioning of the Alliance, the Alliance itself—that is, the fact that in case of general war France, with the means at her disposal, would be at the side of the United States, this being reciprocal, I believe—is beyond question, except in the overworked imaginings (*elucubrations*) of those whose profession it is to alarm honest people by depicting each scratch as an incurable wound.

These declarations are not mere stylish clauses; they are the expression of a political conviction and a political understanding. In regard to Berlin as well as during the Cuban crisis, moreover, the French government has shown exemplary firmness.

No, we should not worry about the manifold consequences of a very problematical—even unthinkable—reversal of alliances, but rather about the more insidious effects of a loosening of Western solidarity. The continuing development of trade and a growing interdependence of interests are not preventing governments from taking larger liberties with regard to their allies and associates. They are pushed in this direction not only by more or less vigorous opposition parties but also by populations whose improved standards of living renders them impatient with the social constraints and discipline implied by any reinforcement of international co-operation. Inequality in prosperity is less easily supported than inequality in mediocrity. Hence a general tendency to press demands which become sharper with the spread of bourgeois values to masses who are left indifferent by ideologies and, consequently, by parties. Governments fearing to be outbid by their adversaries are tempted to maneuver or appease these floating masses by opportunistic policies which sacrifice long-term engagements and sidestep international obligations.

On the other hand, as the Soviet threat seems to recede, one of the factors which helped to join the Atlantic nations loses its influence. The very insistence with which Westerners underline the economic failures of Communist countries and the consequences of advancing polycentrism encourages the hope that the danger has passed. The fear engendered by the permanent presence of ever more terrifying atomic forces is hardly attenuated by the existence of a nuclear balance. A consciousness of the might and the impotence of the two great powers and a feeling that Soviet pressure has allayed combine to stimulate desires for moves that will free the world from the anxieties of war.

In brief, everyone is calling for initiatives. But each conceives these initiatives in function of his estimation of the situation and of his interests. Soviet pressure on Berlin disquieted Washington and London and dissuaded the American and British governments from seeking a negotiated solution with Moscow. The French government, on the contrary, considered it to be a tactical error to negotiate under a threat. American and British leaders are seeking agreements for partial disarmament on arms control and are celebrating the Moscow Treaty of 1963 as an important step toward an international "détente." As for General de Gaulle, he judges that in the absence of a general renunciation of resort to atomic arms, France cannot undertake engagements that will maintain her in a state of inferiority and dependence with regard to atomic powers. But the Paris government does not hesitate to take diplomatic initiatives in the Far East where the United States, directly implicated in a contest of arms, judges negotiations impossible and dangerous. Paris, following London, has just authorized certain commercial transactions with Cuba, thus opening a new breach in the economic blockade, which is the sole arm still at Washington's disposal to enfeeble if not vanquish the Castro regime.

Thus the Western allies face the socialist camp in disarray. They agree neither on strategy nor on a unified diplomatic approach. They have neither common views nor fixed plans for European policy, for a question as important as disengagement, or for Far Eastern policy. It follows that they are not in a position to take advantage of the Sino-Soviet conflict or of that evolution toward polycentrism in the Communist world which they have hailed.

Their policies toward the Third World are scarcely more coherent. Divergences of opinion protrude everywhere. Economic or political rivalries sprout everywhere. English and Americans are not in entire agreement on the attitude to take toward Sukarno. They have not co-ordinated their moves in the Middle East or in the Yemen conflict. In Algeria, where the French are particularly sensitive on the subject of exploiting and transporting Saharan oil, the English and Italians have appeared as competitors in a market the French had thought to reserve. For its part, the French government has not hesitated to encourage the interest certain African members of the Commonwealth have shown in formulas for association with the European Common Market. At the risk of incurring the displeasure

of the United States, France has not hesitated to foster a
French presence in Latin America, thus taking advantage
of the ambiguities arising from the independent stance
affected with regard to her North American ally.

Opinions are just as contradictory on the future of the
Atlantic Alliance, or the future of Europe. The NATO
Council meets, the staffs labor away, the European communities pursue their daily tasks. The Treaty of Rome
is no longer questioned. And yet the Atlantic community
and the "grand design" it was supposed to crown are
hardly discussed anymore. The Kennedy Round is being
approached in a spirit far different from that which underlay the Trade Expansion Act. The United States of Europe
recede on the political horizon. The very principle of integration is disputed, and in paradoxical conditions. By
opposing the admission of Great Britain to the Common
Market, General de Gaulle rejected a useful ally for his
campaign against those "Europeans" who while favoring
integration sought, on the contrary, the admission of a
definite opponent of their policies.

These contradictions have given rise to general confusion. The West has no policy; and the nations of the West,
as a result of being unable to accord their views, paralyze each other, thus dangerously exposing themselves to
the maneuvers that the Soviet Union, China, diverse allies
and Communist parties increasingly embark upon to ag-
gravate these divisions. It is in this progressive loosening
of the ties of the Atlantic Alliance with consequent damage
to the position of the United States and of Europe that the
principal danger for all Western countries and world peace
is to be found. A multiplication of centers of decision,
bringing a proliferation of initiatives, implies in a world
as burdened with various conflicts as ours—conflicts not
easily localized—a serious aggravation of the risk of war.
Through wrong moves by an irresponsible ally, the two
great atomic powers may be confronted at any moment

by the kind of alternative that they fear the most between a major defeat and total war.

It is thus understandable that those responsible for Western policy are uneasily asking themselves how to reverse the current and reinforce their positions.

But if risks are implied in the fluid situation arising from the development of a pluri-polar system, possibilities are no less present, from the very fact that the ideological conflict has lost its virulence and the frontiers between the two camps are not as sharply defined as before. Certainly, the engines of political warfare remain intact. The Soviet Union has not abandoned subversion any more than has China, and countries temper recognition of peaceful co-existence with declarations in support of so-called "just wars"—revolutionary wars and wars of national liberation. A position of permanent defiance constrains China to doctrinal intransigence. But other considerations encourage prudence—consciousness of American power and the desire not to invite catastrophe for a society which after long years of struggle and suffering aspires to well-being. Without doubt Khrushchev remains ready to profit by any occasion offered him by a relaxation in the attention of his enemies. But the Cuban crisis probably taught him to improve his calculations of risks.

In the Cold War which, despite an apparent détente, characterizes relations between East and West, the Communist world disposes of certain trumps. It is better equipped than the West to hide its intentions and to clothe reality with the garments of its choice. But the West is not without means. The Soviet Union has not been in a position to maintain the challenge publicly issued to the capitalist system in the name of the socialist system. Her leaders, like those of Eastern European countries, have had to recognize that their optimistic forecasts have been belied by reality. The continuing confrontation of the two

systems furnishes a demonstration that is not disfavorable
to the West. Levels of development can still be disputed.
But this battle of contradictory and dubious statistics has
lost its political interest. Both sides have acquired a sense
of the relative. No one in the West denies the progress accomplished under a socialist regime in the U.S.S.R., nor the
considerable effort of China, nor even the future possibilities for development of these two great powers. And in the
East, no one thinks any more of denying the impressive
revival of Western Europe and the potential of the American economy, and no one can overlook the force of attraction of the West, confirmed indirectly by the construction
of the Berlin Wall. The Communist world does not dispose
of the economic means to support its pretentions to a
superior system. The countries with planned economies
have a minute share of world trade. Their support to developing countries is very modest by comparison with
what Western Europe and the United States are capable
of providing. Moreover, the public struggle between the
two great Communist powers tarnishes their prestige by
showing that socialist states are just as subject as others
to contradictions arising from personal and national rivalries.

The West should be able to profit by this favorable situation. But it is still necessary that Western leaders be
capable of analyzing, with proper detachment, the fundamental causes of the tensions which are sapping their
strength.

If the central person in the quarrel is General de Gaulle,
it is no less certain that the real debate concerns the fundamental problem of relations between the United States
and Europe, relations between a great power and nations
of lesser or minimal importance, relations not between
equals but between unequals. This problem will not be resolved by ironic remarks on the pursuit of grandeur, by
manifestations of ill temper, or even by a policy of wait-

ing until the troublesome person disappears from the
scene. It would be far better to draw conclusions from the
changes in economic and political stature that have come
about since 1945 and to recognize that the respective positions of Europe and the United States, as well as their
relations with the rest of the world, differ from those existing at the time of the Atlantic pact.

Europe at that time placed herself under the protection
of a power possessing a monopoly or quasimonopoly of the
atomic bomb. Europeans accepted American leadership,
encouraged it, even cultivated it. There is no doubt that
the bad habit of leaving their protection to their American
ally and of bending an ear or holding out a hand to Washington accustomed Washington to making the decisions for
all, and greatly contributed to placing the United States in
the false position of today. For there is no partnership between equals if one of the partners reserves the exclusive
power of life and death for all the associates, which is the
case today. This is why the renewal of the Atlantic Alliance implies that the allies be fully associated with the
decision to resort to atomic weapons. It will be objected,
of course, that if the risks are to be limited, the atomic
club should remain closed; that the American government
is bound by congressional restrictions; that the very
nature of atomic war requires that the decision be delegated to one man and not belong to a group or be made
dependent on the agreement of several governments. The
example of the Cuban crisis will be cited. These arguments are not without value, although the case of a surprise attack should not be confused with the October, 1962,
crisis during which President Kennedy set up a consultative body whose constitution could be envisaged within the
framework of an alliance.

Nevertheless, the solution adopted gives rise to anxiety
and perpetuates uneasiness over whether the man responsible for this awful decision is capable of facing the situa-

tion. Whether intended or not, it transforms allies into satellites or pushes them to develop their own arsenal of atomic arms in order to assure their independence. The problem of political direction will not be solved by association at the level of the multilateral nuclear force. With or without de Gaulle, an Alliance founded on this inequality of power but not of means cannot be viable. If de Gaulle disappears, his successors will sooner or later be tempted to recover by one means or another, with or without the striking force, some form of independence. It suffices to study what Labour leaders envisage as alternatives to the British nuclear force in order to see that, lacking the power to act on the decision to resort to atomic arms, European states will become oriented toward formulas of disengagement or denuclearization intended to prevent their American ally as well as the enemy from using the arms in which they mean to maintain a monopoly. Forces driving in this direction are sufficiently important, in certain European countries such as France, to be heeded.

It also must be admitted that military and economic power is not sufficient to bring about recognition of the preponderant position of the state holding these assets. The reciprocal neutralization of the United States and the Soviet Union has reduced their influence both over their respective allies and the rest of the world, without, however, suppressing fears and suspicions of the powerful. If France today exercises a power of attraction in certain regions of the world, it is without doubt because her President has pursued a marked policy of independence vis-à-vis the United States. But it is also because France is no longer sufficiently powerful to be feared. Is it not striking that the prestige of France and Great Britain in their former colonies has grown proportionately with the reduction of their power to intervene, while the influence of the United States, first among anticolonial powers, has declined with the progress of decolonization? When one or another beneficiary of American aid confronts the American government with certain criticisms, it is not enough to say that the generosity of the American people has gone unrewarded. What warrants attention is the fact that ties between certain former colonies and colonizers have survived revolutionary changes in political relations. Prince Sihanouk may be found disconcerting; but he is not alone in his reactions. If he turns toward France, it is because France offers a prop, even if fragile, permitting him to resist the advance of the Communist world.

Are there not in these demonstrations of sympathy for the France of today some useful pointers for the conduct of Western policy? Would it not be appropriate to analyze more thoroughly the nature of French influence in the Third World? France possesses not only great intellectual prestige. Despite colonial conquests, she has preserved the revolutionary tradition of 1789. Conservative by disposition, she nevertheless continues to represent movement and willing innovation. Outside observers perhaps see France as more to the left than she is. They expect initiatives from her, above all during this period when the two great powers have immobilized each other and while Great Britain appears to be in search of a foreign policy.

The United States saved Europe from nazism and helped the world to free itself of colonialism. But despite the United States' material resources and her talents, despite her vocation as Good Samaritan, she has not succeeded in matching either in Latin America or Africa or Southeast Asia the intellectual ascendancy held by certain European nations. This intellectual ascendancy is an important political factor, above all in regions such as Latin America where students and intellectual circles claim to embody national aspirations and actively intervene in public life. Far from harming the interests of the Atlantic Alliance, a French presence in Mexico, and above all in Brazil, as well as in Africa and the Far East, will on the contrary serve these interests. Because it is not a question, as is sometimes said, of substituting French economic and military aid for the much more considerable support coming from America. The presence of one country does not exclude that of another. It is complementary, even assuring under some circumstances a lightening of the other's burdens. Members of the Atlantic Alliance, and especially the United States as the most heavily burdened, will find every advantage in a distribution of roles according to a division of labor. At a time when Brazil seems to be involved in a crisis the final outcome of which nobody can predict, at a time when the United States is encountering some difficulties in her relations with Latin American countries, is it not desirable that a European ally assure that ties with the West are not broken?

The diversity of means of the Atlantic allies calls for a diversification of roles. It is still necessary, however, to reach a previous understanding on the objectives to be sought and to overcome certain emotional reactions on all sides. It is still necessary to grasp the truth that in relations with the Third World economic power is not as decisive a factor as has been thought—a truth demonstrated even by the success of Soviet and Chinese propaganda. In this period when Alliance ties are loosening, when the contours of the two opposing systems are becoming less distinct, France, whose revolutionary vocation is being renewed by General de Gaulle, can pursue a mission for the West which the United States is not at present in a position to fulfill. Indeed, France has already assumed this role, visibly seeking to break down cold-war barriers outside Europe and to penetrate Soviet positions as well as regions where the Americans have, moreover, invited a European presence. But because French intentions are not understood, the possibilities offered by these moves are not exploited as they could and should be exploited.

As for the European crisis, it cannot be explained either, as we have seen, only by the conflict between a United Kingdom anxious to maintain outside a united Europe special ties with the United States and a France seeking a preponderant position on the continent. There are profounder causes: in particular, national resistance to the process of integration. The construction of a true European state had been hoped for. It was brought to a halt at the halfway point. Circumstances have changed; the institutional approach that was chosen was not the best. One ought to ask if it would not be appropriate to become more pragmatic and to follow the recommendations that the European federalists themselves made at their 1947 Congress of Montreux. Differences opposing some of the most convinced supporters of today's "little Europe" and those favoring a "large Europe" arise not so much over the final objective of reinforcement of European co-operation. At most, disputes over objectives concern the form of the political institutions that must complete the European structure, the necessity of a bicameral system, the respective roles of the chambers, the balance of powers— although this kind of discussion involves a too distant and too uncertain future to provoke any other than speculative interest.

No, opposition arises chiefly over methods. The federalists who are functionalists are convinced that Europe can be built only if diversity is accepted, that it is thus a question—and here they are not very far from the views of General de Gaulle—of working with the states as they exist today, with states among which collaboration must be steadily increased as needs and circumstances command. European unity will not come about through the imposition of a political system previously elaborated by a few specialists in constitutional law. It will come about through a convergence of interests. If a nation of Europe is to become a reality, it must be open to all possible candidates, not only to members of EFTA, but eventually also to East European nations. If the Six have performed a signal service by forming a European nucleus and by constraining other nations to define their position with regard to that nucleus, they have at the same time, through a certain doctrinal intransigence, held back progress toward unity and reinforced the frontiers to the East at the very moment when opportunities for new contacts arose. Can it not be seen that it might be rewarding to maintain or even reinforce ties with a Finland situated by geography and historical circumstances at the borders of two antagonistic systems? Why not make a special place for neutral Austria, for that borderline country at the portals of Danubian and Balkan Europe?

For that matter, why not break paths toward such countries as Hungary, Czechoslovakia, and Rumania, not to speak of Poland, a country with a tradition of close ties with Western Europe? And this should be done not with the aim of toppling the regimes in power, but rather of encouraging an apparent evolution toward a relaxation of constraints and more flexible policies, and thus of favoring the necessary détente. It is perhaps in Prague and Budapest as well as in Moscow that the solution to the Berlin problem will be found today.

Without a doubt the development of economic and cultural ties with Eastern European countries incurs risks because the engines of political warfare have not been dismantled. But considering the permanent threat posed by the atomic arms race and at the same time the perspectives opened by the evolution of the Communist world toward polycentrism, the risks are worth taking, The West hardly has a choice. Facing attacks from all sides, it must know that it cannot afford, over the long run, the luxury of a simultaneous struggle against the socialist camp and against the advancing demands of the so-called developing nations. At the present time it would seem less difficult to relax slightly relations with certain countries belonging to the socialist system than to resolve the formidable problem posed by underdevelopment.

In this world sliding toward an anarchy which could lead to catastrophe, it is without doubt difficult to make predictions and even more so to make suggestions. Taking account of circumstances which are perhaps temporary, one can at most attempt to distinguish the directions in which, eventually, the principal effort should be made. Before making such an effort, however, Western countries must be able to agree on the content, the orientation, and methods of Western policy. That is why there are no more urgent tasks than those of renewing unity by reintegrating France in the Atlantic Alliance and of putting an end to the quarrel between the two Europes. Only then will the West be in a position to devote its material and intellectual resources to the service of peace.

The Future
of the Alliance:
A Pragmatic Approach

by

*Laurence W. Martin**

It is inevitable that the Western Alliance, being a product of the Cold War, must change in shape as that dominating tension relaxes, tightens, or shifts its thrust. Evolutionary crises have been a consistent feature of NATO as, like any traditional coalition of states, it has adjusted to variations in the balance of advantages it confers on its members. A certain skepticism is therefore justified when observers identify each successive adaptation as a decisive turning point. The conjuncture of events we face in the mid-sixties, however, does indeed seem to mark the true end of the postwar era and the start of a new stage in the organization of the West.

Several elements can be distinguished contributing to a new sense of fluidity in face of what is widely believed to

* *Laurence W. Martin:* Associate Professor of International Politics, School of Advanced International Studies, The Johns Hopkins University. Author of *Peace without Victory*; co-author with Arnold Wolfers of *The Anglo-American Tradition in Foreign Affairs*; editor of *Neutralism and Nonalignment*.

be the end of bipolarity, the dawn of polycentrism, and the substitution of a balance of maneuver for what has so long been a rigid confrontation of blocs. Of these novel elements the one most directly relevant to the organization of the West is the economic, political, and moral resurgence of Western Europe, in defense of which the Alliance was originally created. A second novelty has been the recognition by both the Soviet Union and the United States of their nuclear vulnerability, mutual if not equal, leading to an apparent strategic deadlock and consequent parallel declarations by both nations that major war can no longer be an instrument of active policy. Arising in part from this recognition is a third novelty in today's world, the emergence of a language of détente between Russia and America and the perception by many Europeans and Americans of an important change for the better in Russian purposes and tactics.

These developments combine to mark a distinctive pattern in affairs; each also has its particular consequence. The rise of Europe, which would, for example, be significant even in the absence of détente, calls into question the balance of the Alliance; the strategic deadlock questions the adequacy of the Alliance; the apparent détente questions the need for it.

An initial appreciation of this state of world affairs might suggest it marks the triumph and fulfillment of NATO—Russia contained, Western Europe free, prosperous, and at peace with itself. Reflection, however, brings a deeper failure to light, for it was originally intended that such achievements would also produce a legitimate settlement in the center and a liberation in the East of Europe. A firm Western stand was to bring about Soviet withdrawal, whether inspired by necessity in face of superior power or by a slow change of heart. Either event could free the United States from its European entanglement: Either Russia would become amenable to President Roose-

velt's conception of a concert or a revivified Europe
would become capable of containing Russia alone. Much
of the current confused debate in the Alliance concerns
the degree to which our merely partial successes justify
our acting as though our full original hopes had been fulfilled.

The stakes of such debate are high indeed. East-West
conflict is frozen rather than resolved, perhaps a natural
outcome in an era when wars are prepared but not fought.
The process of dismantling such a conflict is less akin to
traditional peacemaking than to negotiation of an armistice with an adversary still powerful in the field, fraught
with dangers of disrupting alignments with one's allies, of
unsteadying one's forces, and of presenting the foe with
the temptation of unexpected opportunities.

Some are now willing to rate the risks of such a process
low and to proceed to dismantle the Western Alliance.[1]
Such a view requires a high estimate of Europe's military
and diplomatic capacities and little expectation of renewed Soviet adventurism. Those most bored with the
burdens of Cold War or who stand to gain most from the
relaxation of Atlantic ties naturally find their calculations
arriving at answers to justify such optimism. From the
American point of view such calculations must concern not
merely European capacity to assume greater control of
Western foreign policy but the probability of its doing so
in ways congenial to the United States.

The prevailing American opinion is that those who would
now dismantle the Alliance underestimate the extent to
which modifications of Soviet behavior arise from a Western position of strength to which intimate American co-
operation with Europe is still vital. Stabilization and
détente have not descended upon us gratuitously; they

[1] For a thoroughgoing statement of this view, see Ronald Steel, *The
End of Alliance: America and the Future of Europe* (New York:
Viking, 1964).

have been built on a balance of effort and must with effort be maintained. The fat and pacific Soviet Communist is a devoutly awaited prophesy; he is not yet fully manifest. Russian belts are undoubtedly looser but they are assuredly not beyond retightening. Nor, indeed, have Russians at their present girth proved too portly for considerable mischief. Multipolarity is thus the product of a continued underlying bipolarity. The newfound latitude of the medium powers is a function not only of their own regained substance but also in large part of the overriding Russian-American balance. It is therefore essential to insure that efforts to adapt to hopeful diplomatic and strategic changes do not impair the conditions, in particular the Western position of strength, from which those changes flow.

There seems no reason to fear that a cautious response to relaxation of tension will in itself impair the interest of the other side in détente, provided grossly provocative acts are avoided. For the most convincingly identified sources of Soviet moderation—the economic and technological superiority of the West, the growing demands of Soviet internal development, the rise of China—are not readily reversible at Russian will. Thus while the West should be prepared to acquiesce in steps to stabilize the effects of these incentives to Soviet moderation, it does not have to make concessions to create the incentives themselves.

American interests in the Western Alliance today consequently call for maintaining a strong military balance against Russia in Europe, and for continuing to seek the original goal of a legitimate settlement in Central Europe. It is also an American interest that its allies refrain from dangerous adventures, an interest that entails a cautious approach to nuclear questions and to satisfaction of German territorial grievances. Outside Europe the United States needs all the help it can secure in executing its

world-wide responsibilities. This chiefly means participation in economic development and in international polic-
ing.

All these interests are the concerns that have become traditional to the American role as grand marshal of the Alliance. Now it is necessary to recognize that the improvement in the economic condition of Europe and impairment
in that of America, however temporary, make it increasingly likely that the United States must give new attention
to intrinsic interests of its own, and that the day when the
United States could welcome behavior inimical to its own
economic welfare, so long as it strengthened other members of the Alliance, is probably over.

The patterns of relationship between America and its
allies that can serve these interests are infinite in detail
but fairly limited in principle. One possibility is a perpetuation of the initial configuration of a dominant United
States surrounded by a coalition of more or less compliant
allies. This configuration could conceivably be continued
though some of the allies would inevitably be more powerful and more assertive than hitherto. At the other extreme
the United States could enter a more or less equal partnership with resurgent Europe, a Europe that would almost
certainly dispose of its own nuclear power. In this pattern
which, roughly speaking, is the famed "dumbbell," the
connecting link could be of strengths varying from close
co-ordination to the most casual co-operation. The Europe
in question might also vary from the supranational entity
envisaged by the federalists to a looser coalition of father-
lands. Any of these Europes might embrace more or
fewer of the European nations and those outside might
either continue an allied relationship or retire into a growing body of neutrals. As a third possibility, quite novel
patterns may emerge for the West, perhaps with the
framework varying from function to function, now loose,
now tight, now comprehensive, now limited to a core of

nations, thereby leaving open the door for such presently unconceived notions as may later emerge for our emerging pluralist yet interdependent world.

For the moment the United States has recognized the erosion of its old style hegemony and is exploring ways of working out a more apparently equal relation to a coalescing Europe. The heart of the debate that has proceeded on how to do this has concerned the disposition of strategic nuclear weapons. Having for so long put most of its discourse in nuclear terms America cannot well protest the application of similar tests by others. The key question is, of course, whether nuclear forces in American hands, hitherto mainstay of the Alliance, can continue to receive European acceptance as an adequate deterrent against direct aggression or indirect assaults on European interests. This is a question not only of whether such a deterrent can be efficient and reliable but also of whether it can be extended in ways compatible with the self-respect of nations now enjoying an increased sense of their own importance and with the degree of diplomatic influence they conceive to be their due.

The old question, latent since Russia acquired a nuclear armory, as to whether nuclear technology and alliances are fundamentally compatible, is thus posed with increasing urgency. In outline, the strategical debate is widely understood. American threats to retaliate with a nuclear attack on Russia in the event of an otherwise irresistible Soviet attack on Western Europe lose in credibility as the United States itself becomes vulnerable. Many before de Gaulle pointed out that suicidal threats are impressive, if ever, only from entities with a strong sense of self or oneness. The response of American military leaders under Secretary of Defense Robert McNamara has been to prepare a flexible strategy, with a scheme for counterforce bargaining by nuclear weapons short of massive annihilation, and with a build-up of conventional forces capable of meeting sizable attacks without any nuclear measures at all. This strategic doctrine, however, already much modified since first pronouncement, has raised almost as many doubts as it has allayed in European minds, which fear that the necessary flexibility may be secured at their expense. These fears range from simple misgivings that the very search for such a policy confirms the infirmity of American purpose to the more refined anxiety that targets for counterforce action may be in Western Europe, arriving at a situation in which tolerable use of nuclear weapons will be defined as use upon targets not in the territory of the two nuclear superpowers.

Similar misgivings surround the plan for increased conventional forces. Preparing a conventional defense, think many Europeans, means preparing to fight a destructive campaign on their soil. This, though doubtless better than thermonuclear war, if it has to come, is still not as attractive an alternative as it is for Americans. Moreover, there are fears that conventional preparedness increases the risk of war by reducing credibility of the massive deterrent. Such fears explain in part why some European nations have emphasized the early use of tactical nuclear weapons while maintaining a doctrine of ready escalation, the resolution of the paradox being, of course, that they rely heavily on nuclear weapons as a deterrent precisely because they believe their use as a defense would be intolerable.

The "pure" solution for European uncertainties, the proliferation of national deterrents, is generally regarded in the United States as undesirable and improbable for reasons already well debated. Such policies are not open to many of the allies for technical reasons, and the capacity of even the major members to sustain large nuclear efforts is much questioned. It is not absolutely clear that future technological developments will all militate against small nuclear forces. Some believe the contrary to be true. But the prevailing position of the American government at present is that projected European programs are militarily ineffective and, worse than ineffective, dangerous as accident-prone interferences with the control of response that can alone preserve the credibility of deterrence.

The dangers of proliferation, were it possible, may have been exaggerated. A direct correlation between a rise in the number of nuclear centers and an increased danger of catastrophe cannot be conclusively demonstrated. But in any case, the likelihood of proliferation seems only superficially to be likely. There are few signs that any new members of the coalition are contemplating such a departure. The most vexed question is the case of Germany. Here the legal, technical, political, diplomatic, and geographical obstacles the Germans would face are formidable. The prospect of German access to strategic nuclear weapons, even in indirect forms, undoubtedly does arouse fears both in the West and, quite genuinely, in Eastern Europe. Present German interest appears to be directed more to securing assurance as to the general nuclear strategy of the Alliance than to setting out on the road to nuclear sovereignty. Nevertheless, the long-term prospects must remain in doubt, and even if proliferation in Europe were not itself destabilizing, it might ripple out as a precedent for other areas.

On the other hand, the "pure" solution and the one simplest from the American point of view—complete surrender of Western nuclear efforts to the control of the United States—is almost certainly unattainable. In addition to the strategic case for independent European nuclear capacity, a number of other considerations serve to keep European interest in nuclear weapons alive. So long as each exists, the French and British programs feed on each other, neither nation being likely to concede the sole European nuclear role to the other. Nor are Western European countries likely to surrender the prestige that participation in nuclear matters confers, the leverage upon the United States, the access to negotiation on nuclear questions, the possible commercial advantages of keeping up with an important branch of modern technology, or some nuclear option for the future in the event the whole shape of the technical and political world changes again.[2]

Appreciating the force of these considerations, recent U.S. administrations have been busily engaged in exploration of hybrid alternatives. Crudely put, the task here, from the American vantage point, is to give Europeans as much of the appearance of nuclear participation and as little of the substance of nuclear decision as will persuade them not to adopt policies that are incompatible with American strategic doctrine. No one can predict with certainty what arrangements would fulfill such an essentially psychological purpose. So long as Europeans proceed rationally, however—and for each European nation the rationale will vary somewhat—they need assurance that nuclear weapons will be available for their defense when necessary, that the Soviet Union is impressed by this, and that if they have to be used the weapons will be employed in ways least harmful to European interests. This means taking care of targets dangerous to Europe—Soviet medium-range ballistic missile (MRBM) sites in western Russia, for example—in a "clean" fashion and avoiding any unnecessary nuclear fire, from friend or foe, on Western Europe. Ideally, Europeans also need safeguards against American action in any other part of the world—particularly nuclear action—that might expose them to attack

---

[2] See, for instance, the rather vehement refusal of Viscount Hailsham to abandon "all the advanced and sophisticated technologies" quoted by Governor Rockefeller in his February 9, 1963, press conference, and the thought-provoking assertion by Douglas-Hume at Ottawa in May, 1963, that "We have decided that Britain must be equipped to be present in the councils of war and peace—and to be there by right. And this means nuclear power."

when they do not themselves believe their vital interests are at stake.

Neither Americans nor Europeans are likely to achieve a full measure of their demands within a collective system. So long as they remain separate political entities it can never be wholly satisfying to leave even a portion of vital decisions in other hands. Efforts to approximate a solution have ranged from sharing information on existing policy, to consulting on the design, deployment, and contingency planning of nuclear forces, and, finally, to a share in deciding when to employ such weapons. Somewhere along this continuum appears the question of whether it is necessary for others than the United States to own or have complete custody of the actual nuclear weapons.

The ins and outs of schemes for collective nuclear activity are manifold and complex. Many forms of limited bilateral and multilateral sharing and coordination already exist. Most ambitious of new proposals is the vexed scheme for a multimanned seaborne force of Polaris submarines. This is not the place to take up the history and merits of the MLF itself, but it seems fair to say that in its officially proposed form it falls into the traditional pattern of the Alliance within which the United States remains the dominant partner with a substantial nuclear hegemony. The Europeans secure a veto over use of the joint force but arrangements so far suggested give them neither a positive power to launch the force nor any control over the use made by America of its remaining preponderant national forces. American hegemony would be complete if proponents of MLF were vindicated in their scarcely veiled hope that the attractions of the force will kill European national deterrents on the vine. Yet some recent theories that Soviet ICBM's might be able to deter massive American retaliation, while Soviet MRBM's held Europe hostage against a Western counterforce strategy, tend to support the case for at least a finite countercity force in European hands.[3]

Aware of the shortcomings in many European eyes of this military arrangement and of the political relationship it implies, other proponents of the MLF who are devoted to the ideal of European unity conceive the force in a different way. By hints of control by majority vote they present MLF as the route to an independent deterrent under joint European control. This would indeed, they believe, have sufficient magnetism to kill off the national forces. In this perspective the MLF appears to envisage not the perpetuation of the old integrated alliance under American hegemony but the starting point of a true "dumbbell" configuration.

The most effective single public American encouragement for this notion of a nuclear partnership was probably McGeorge Bundy's speech at Copenhagen in September, 1962, when he said "we ourselves cannot usurp from the new Europe the responsibility for deciding in its own way the level of effort and of investment which it wishes to make in these great matters." [4] Some who endorse this attitude do so from the belief that a unified Europe not only can, but must, by nature, dispose of all the instruments of power. This notion has been voiced by Pierre Messmer, by such a non-Gaullist as Jean Monnet, and by Edward Heath, who gave one of the most detailed expositions when, in the full flood of negotiations for British entry into the EEC, he declared:

> We quite accept that the European political union, if it is to be effective, will have a common concern for defense problems and that a European point of view will emerge. . . . Of course, as the European Community develops, the balance within the Atlantic Alliance is

---

[3] Cf. Philip Windsor, *Western Europe in Soviet Strategy* (London: Adelphi Paper, 1964).

[4] Speech before Atlantic Treaty Association, September 27, 1962.

going to change. In the course of time there will be two great groups in the West: North America and Europe. The growth of the European point of view in the defense field will not, we believe, be long in making itself felt.[5]

There is little doubt that Europe could support a considerable nuclear force. With American co-operation it could quite rapidly be realized. What makes the discussion academic is, of course, the fact that no Europe exists, or is likely to exist soon, that would be capable of creating, far less operating, a European deterrent. The existing "Six," and still more the Six with Britain and her followers added, are unlikely to have more than a rudimentary political organization in the near future, and the whole problem of the Alliance is the incompatability of loose political structures and nuclear policy. It is certainly conceivable that a nuclear force could be the center around which community might be built. But it seems unlikely. Past experience suggests nuclear matters are more divisive than solidifying and, as in the Alliance as a whole, federal structures demand explicitness in areas sometimes best spared too minute a scrutiny.

What is of more immediate interest is the vision of a future structure for the Western bloc that underlies the advocacy of a united Europe, including Britain, and acting as a diplomatic, economic, and military unit at the highest level. Many have been attracted by the idea of America acquiring a single European partner, thereby basing the Alliance on what have been called the "two pillars." Such a dualism, indeed, usually seems to be what is meant by the slogan of "partnership," and many of the advocates of Atlantic community complete with institutions believe it

---

[5] Speech to the Council of Western European Union, April 10, 1962.

can come about only by the approximation of Europe and America as equals.[6]

This prospect suits those in America whose view of Europe, consciously or not, is a projection of American experience, so that their solutions for problems of co-operation in the free world partake of the nature of state-building with an ultimately federal mold for the whole Atlantic area. Others believe that only equals can whole-heartedly co-operate, and that a united Europe offers the sole prospect of an equal associate for America. The solution to the problem of American predominance must be the end of predominance, though perhaps not all advocates of the two pillars phrase it this way themselves. Creation of Greater Europe also has the definitiveness and tidiness that appeals to many Americans in their approach to po-litical questions; to the aspect of American foreign policy that thinks of diplomacy in terms of establishing and run-ning "operations" rather than manipulating autonomous entities. In this sense, pushing Britain into the EEC would have removed the complication of dealing with an impor-tant unit that did not fit the preconceived scheme. Nor can it be forgotten that, for some, the vision of a united Europe revived prospects of ultimate disengagement from trans-Atlantic problems that originally underlay NATO and the Marshall Plan.

The merits of the two pillars design for the Western bloc depend in large part on the nature of the pillars and their probable mutual relations. Recent events have made it clear that, for the time being, the design fails—as in the

---

[6] See, for example, André Philip: "To have a dialogue there must first be two and not an anarchic crowd."—"Socialism, Neutralism, Pacifism," *Atlantic Community Quarterly*, March, 1963, p. 71. More recently, the official communiqué of the Johnson-Erhard meeting in Texas declared (December 29, 1963): "The President and the Chan-cellor agreed that the central requirements in the policy of the West must be to increase the strength and effectiveness of the emerging Atlantic partnership. They reaffirmed their conviction that an in-creasingly unified Europe is vital to this effort."

strategic field—because there is little prospect of the European pillar being erected. The problems the Six face with their existing degree of co-operation make a Europe capable of acting with a cohesion comparable to the United States seem even more remote than when the ideologues of Atlantic community first seized on it.

This leaves open, however, the question of whether the United States should continue to put pressure on Europe to unite with a view to producing a political partner in the future. Events have made it difficult not to notice that a United Europe might prove a recalcitrant partner. Concern about one aspect of this is expressed in the frequent exhortations that Europe be "outward looking," by which rather loose phrase it is meant that she should be a liberal trader and a reasonable negotiating partner willing to shoulder burdens of the Alliance and tailor its policies to the broader concept of the free world. A cynic might more briefly define outward looking as ready to fall in with the grand designs of Washington.

It is now obvious such complaisance is not to be taken for granted. Most now agree that, whatever his idiosyncrasies, General de Gaulle's self-assertiveness represents a pervasive though by no means inevitably dominant streak in European opinion. To this way of thinking, "interdependence" is an abhorrent idea, especially if it is a euphemism for American leadership. Even a cautious Canadian observer, trying to promote co-operation, comments, "It is strange how few Americans have recognized the deep-seated anti-American aspects of the European movement, the urge to be independent of American aid and American policy. . . ." [7] One source of this blindness seems to have been the impression that the EEC was chiefly about free trade, while it is really concerned with economic growth, community building, social planning,

---

[7] John Holmes, "Implications of the European Economic Community," *Atlantic Community Quarterly,* March, 1963, p. 31.

and self-respect. The question therefore becomes whether a European political community, capable of equal partnership, can be created at a level of self-willed deviation from American guidance compatible with the degree of coordination regarded as essential by the United States. This being far from certain, it is not impossible that a loosely knit Greater Europe might be more serviceable than a coherent but recalcitrant unity that excluded many of America's long-term allies.

One theory behind partnership is that only equals can co-operate freely. But it can be argued with equal force that there are real differences of interest between Europe and the United States—some economic, some arising from the tasks of community building, some from competition for primacy in dealing with the single adversary, yet others from the inevitable divergencies of strategic view that geography imposes—and that these would be compounded by synthesis into a single center of responsibility disposing of the resources to attempt an independent course. The argument that only equals can co-operate can thus be countered with the thesis that divergent interests become irresistible when the parties concerned have pretensions to self-sufficiency. All this leaves unexplored misgivings expressed about the effects of uniting Western Europe on the chance of moving closer to Eastern Europe, and in particular of rendering relations between the two Germanies more intimate.

As such possibilities emerge Washington displays increasing concern for the strength of the link between the two halves of the dumbbell. The machinery for this link is rarely detailed, but the substance of the relationship seems to be that views acceptable to Americans as to how to conduct world affairs should prevail in the Western camp. Since it is hard to conceive of ways in which even good behavior in the present could guarantee conduct in the future, it is easy to see why many Europeans suspect the institutional arrangements proposed are intended to disguise and perpetuate American predominance.

Doubts about the amenability of the European pillar are now fairly widely entertained in America. Much less often is it acknowledged that the American pillar may also be unready for partnership. The existence of a great American center of power and decision is not of course in doubt. But it is equally clear that the United States has no real intention of trammeling its formal independence or reducing itself to merely an Atlantic partner. That is to say that while the United States would like a firm arch between the two pillars to constrain Europe from using its newly united power in ways inimical to American interests, it is unwilling to restrict its own freedom reciprocally. Traffic on the arch would be one-way. All the more remote then are elaborate schemes for true Atlantic federalism on other than the most rarified, symbolic level.

The question arises therefore as to whether it is even wise to encourage the development of such symbolism as the proponents of Atlantic community have done. America is an Atlantic power only in an inclusive and certainly not an exclusive sense. The United States has a global role peculiar to herself, in which she has no presently conceivable equal partner, and in which for the moment her only true opposite number is the Soviet Union.

Regardless of all the nuclear possibilities discussed previously the United States remains the Grand Deterrer. Whatever progress the Europeans may make in the next few years, the possibility of American nuclear action, however watered by doubt, will pose by far the most weighty uncertainties faced by Soviet strategists in Europe. All European plans, including those of General de Gaulle, accept this as part of the world within which they intend to pursue their own policies.[8] In addition, America's power is engaged in many areas of the world where few Europeans are still concerned. The United States cannot submit its actions in these areas to European consent without encouraging a lowest common denominator of resistance to Communist initiative that would gradually permeate all diplomacy as well as the directly military confrontation.

As the great deterrer, as a Pacific power, indeed as the only truly world power now existing in the democratic camp, the United States cannot accept Europe as an equal partner so long as it remains essentially local. Indeed, does encouraging the coagulation of Europe render an unqualified service to the American goal of a pluralistic order for the entire non-Communist world? Is it wise to encourage the remaining European nations that profess a concern for global affairs to submerge their identity in a more parochial community; to insist, for instance, on extinguishing a distinct British voice in the Alliance? Might it not be more valuable to preserve an associate, however junior, with a world-wide presence to share in the public accounting for such operations as the recent aid to India, to show an interest and a presence east of Suez, and to act as an informed critic on matters so removed from the concerns of Brussels?

The conclusion emerges that dominant American leadership is henceforth inevitably open to question and that solutions centered around the Atlantic alone, especially on federalist models, are both remote and of doubtful merit. Consideration of economic policies or of the details of diplomatic tactics in the Cold War lead to much the same conclusions as are drawn from the military realm. For the reasons sketched in this paper, and for many others, the

---

[8] Thus one can probably take seriously—all the more for its tart phrasing—the General's remark in his July 30, 1963, press conference: "en cas de guerre générale la France, avec les moyens qu'elle a, serait aux côtes des États-Unis, et je crois reciproquement."

United States cannot resolve the tensions occasioned by its primacy in the Alliance by conjuring up Europe in an effort to shed its predominance. On the contrary, America must remain the prime and most widely extended member of the Western grouping for the foreseeable future, and this will be symbolized by its retention of overwhelming nuclear force.

The United States must therefore resign itself to an untidier coalition than is perhaps congenial to the American political genius. In a sense the design for Atlantic community fails, not because it is ahead of its time, but because it reflects too much the shape of the past. It seeks to perpetuate the pattern of the last two wars in which America has come to help the Western extremities of Europe in an essentially European conflict. Even in the last war this perspective called forth charges of neglect for other theaters. If Europe is still undoubtedly the most important player, stake, and area in the game, it is certainly not the whole picture. Already the various neutrals, the Commonwealth, the incongruous appearance of Japan in OECD all serve as reminders of the loose ends a solely Atlantic formula entails.

Perhaps we must fall back on the third alternative mentioned at the outset, abandon the discourse of pillars and communities, with its connotation of well-defined structure, and work toward *ad hoc* functional systems—some military, some economic, some tight, some loose—not as a mere second best but as a flexible framework that would do most to meet the demands of the present without prejudicing the possibilities of the future interdependent world. Such a framework might avoid the demands of logical precision which constitutional schemes demand but which are not necessarily well-suited to the uncertainties and probabilities of modern strategic systems or the ramifications of international economic relations.

As a limited expedient for solution of Germany's peculiar

problem, and as a vehicle for expanded co-operation and consultation, a device like the MLF, for example, may well have a place in such a framework. But there is no need to regard it as a blueprint for the future of the West. It is not yet obvious that the groupings available for particular military purposes are those best suited to the long-term political future. Yet unless this is freely recognized, hastily erected structures may become obstacles to other ventures. Even as a strictly military matter, elaborate schemes need not entail rejection of more limited forms of co-operation. The best hope may therefore be for something in the nature of a jointly operated force akin to MLF to accommodate Germany, with the British and French nuclear forces surviving, formally independent but in practice increasingly integrated, as a specialized contribution to common power. In the same spirit improvements in the consultative arrangements for broader matters and for the formulation of strategic doctrine could be built by those who chose to do so.

A loose constellation of this kind would call for more rather than less quality in American leadership. Leadership must mean resignation to interminable frustration and the final abandonment of the belief that somewhere there exists a way to transcend the perpetual wrestle with problems never susceptible to complete solution. The right to cut the knots of allied indecision, in the last resort, can only be gracefully retained, if at all, by virtue of inexhaustible patience with associates, deference for their views, and tenderness for their interests.

Analogies with the deference of the superior to the inferior in the Commonwealth that resulted in the free entry of the Dominions to two world wars are tempting but perhaps farfetched. One feature of British experience is relevant however. The now much derided "special relationship" was no complete illusion, as any familiarity with the intimacy and mutual confidence of British and American officials, compared to their continental opposites, will confirm. In essence, by co-operation, the British purchased a close hearing whenever they felt obliged to dig in their toes on a truly vital interest. The skill the British showed in cultivating this relationship is often acknowledged. Curiously, Americans have been slow to recognize it as a considerable achievement on their part too.

By its nature, the special relationship cannot be extended to others without dilution. But the adjective and the noun are not completely inseparable. If "specialness" is not very extendable, the substance of the relation may be more elastic. It should not be impossible to develop among the leading allies something of the same sense of being less than foreign to each other, the confidence that their major interests are consistently and sympathetically taken into account, not from time to time, but as a natural part of the daily workings of American government. Some, it is true, would reject such intimacy, but it is not easy to believe we have yet exhausted the possibilities in this direction. Should the United States succeed in establishing such patterns it might find itself, as Sir Winston Churchill once envisaged Britain, at the intersection of a set of varied circles describing the wide orbit of its interests.

Index